CELEBRATING THE LORD'S SUPPER

Celebrating the Lord's Supper is a very refreshing and thought-provoking work that challenges one's thinking about the place and significance of the Lord's Supper for the Christian church, especially in Africa. The book poses an apt challenge to the African church to reflect deeply and make the gospel real in its context. That "It is high time for us to find practical ways in which the Lord's Supper can be inculturated in socio-cultural groups across Africa" is a most passionate appeal that cannot be ignored.

It is a challenge to our thinking both in African Christian theology and in the development of African liturgy that truly reflects the distinctive cultural experiences of African worshippers. Doing this without abandoning biblical principles is important. This book is relevant to all, and scholars and pastors will have a lot to interact with. Even if you have a divergent opinion, Dr Edison Kalengyo has started a discussion that cannot be ignored and raised an issue that is significant for spiritual development.

I am grateful to Dr Kalengyo for this approach, and for articulating this issue of the Lord's Supper succinctly. With this we shall continue to engage. More significant about this work is that it is written by an African living in Africa and for the African peoples. Thus, it is authentic and I warmly commend it.

The Rt Rev Stephen Ayodeji A. Fagbemi, PhD
Bishop, Anglican Diocese of Owo, Nigeria

As Edison Kalengyo makes clear, there is a spiritual famine across Africa because so few of the Lord's people are being fed at the communion table. With a pastor's heart and a theologian's depth and clarity, he uncovers not only the causes for this famine but many practical and biblically sound approaches to its remedy. This brief, lively and very readable book belongs in the hands of every pastor and pastor-to-be on the continent. It is African theology at its best.

Joel A. Carpenter, PhD
Director, Nagel Institute for the Study of World Christianity
Calvin College, Grand Rapids, MI, USA

CELEBRATING THE LORD'S SUPPER

ENDING THE EUCHARISTIC FAMINE

Edison Muhindo Kalengyo

Published 2018 by HippoBooks, an imprint of ACTS and Langham Publishing.

Africa Christian Textbooks (ACTS), TCNN, PMB 2020, Bukuru 930008, Plateau State, Nigeria. **www.actsnigeria.org**

Langham Publishing, PO Box 296, Carlisle, Cumbria CA3 9WZ, UK
www.langham.org

ISBNs:
978-1-78368-409-0 Print
978-1-78368-410-6 ePub
978-1-78368-411-3 Mobi
978-1-78368-412-0 PDF

British Library Cataloguing-in-Publication Data
A catalogue record for this book is available from the British Library

ISBN: 978-1-78368-409-0

Cover & Book Design: projectluz.com

I dedicate this book to my beloved wife Dorothy
who has remained an invaluable friend and partner
in my pastoral and theological journey

CONTENTS

FOREWORD

In the past, it might have taken weeks, months, or even years before we heard that famine had struck a community. These days, we get the news almost immediately. Yet there is an insidious famine we have missed: People not only hunger for food, they also hunger for the word of God and for the Lord's Supper (the Eucharist). This is what Associate Professor Edison Muhindo Kalengyo describes as "an unacknowledged famine" – many faithful Christians are starving because they are not receiving the Eucharist.

I have been deeply engaged with the theological and pastoral problem of the eucharistic famine for a number of years. It first came to my attention when I was asked by Stephen Noll, then Vice Chancellor of Uganda Christian University, to review a book by my own professor, Professor Peter G. Bolt, who together with other eminent theologians had published *The Lord's Supper in Human Hands*. That book showed me that the Lord's Supper is a deep theological and pastoral matter that is critical to our understanding of the gospel. Faithful believers must receive the Eucharist but, as Dr Kalengyo reminds us, a large part of our congregations today are living without feeding on the Eucharist. Yet this is something that Christ commanded, telling his disciples "Do this in remembrance of me."

Dr Kalengyo's book, *Celebrating the Lord's Supper*, will not only be of help to pastors and lay Christians but will also be theologically and pastorally transforming for many who read it. I recommend it with a prayer that it will bring many in Africa to a better understanding of the sacrificial nature of the Eucharist.

May God bless this book to the encouragement of many thousands and open doors for many faithful Christians who have been starved from the Eucharist.

Rt Rev Dr Alfred Olwa,
Bishop, Diocese of Lango, Uganda,
January 2018

PREFACE

In the life of the Christian church, the Lord's Supper remains the central Christian ritual in which the life, death and resurrection of Jesus Christ are celebrated. Yet current rules governing the celebration of the Lord's Supper have divided the church in Africa into two groups: the eucharistically privileged few and the eucharistically underprivileged majority, who remain excluded from the Lord's Table. This situation is aptly described as an endemic famine of the Lord's Supper.

My passion is to work to alleviate this famine, and so in this book I address its causes and offer some solutions. I also make an urgent plea for contextual celebration of the Lord's Supper that will enhance our understanding and appreciation of the meaning and significance of the death of Christ.

It is my sincere hope and prayer that this book will be a useful resource for pastors, teachers, lay readers and Christians for the foreseeable future.

To God be the Glory.

Edison Muhindo Kalengyo
2018

ACKNOWLEDGEMENTS

A completed work like this bears the imprint of many hands. I am thankful to the Langham Partnership, Ridley Hall (Cambridge), and the All Africa Conference of Churches (AACC), Nairobi, for providing resources and space for my sabbatical leave in 2011 and 2012. Uganda Christian University was generous in granting me time for research. The Nagel Institute (Calvin College) offered me an opportunity as a visiting scholar in 2016 that enabled me to put together a publishable manuscript. I am also thankful to the publishers who helped to refine the manuscript and facilitate publication and distribution. I particularly wish to acknowledge my consultant editor, Isobel Stevenson, of Langham Partnership. With unequalled patience she worked tirelessly and selflessly to put the material in a flowing, readable form.

In all this, my wife Dorothy and my children (Mwesigwa, Alinda and Ahebwa) have stood by me, and I have benefited immensely from their fervent prayers and moral support.

1

AN UNACKNOWLEDGED FAMINE

Africa, my beloved continent, is constantly the focus of international news and attention; often for the wrong reasons. It seems to me that the international media like it that way, for when something good happens on the African continent, it receives little or no international media attention. You do not have to labour to convince anybody in the West that Africa is a continent of chronic famine, hunger, war, conflict – the list is endless.

People in the West should not be blamed for their distorted perception of Africa and African peoples. That is how aid agencies constantly portray Africa in order to attract funding. That is the Africa people see on their television screens. They are fed a diet of images of starving children in South Sudan, Ethiopia, Somalia and other parts of Africa.

But there is one particular category of famine the media never report. Yet to me it is the famine of all famines. It is the famine endured by the faithful in Africa. Here I am not talking about a lack of physical food but a lack of spiritual food. People are hungry, starving, for want of the Lord's Supper. Deeply moved by this widespread famine, some Kenyan priests made the following emotional pastoral appeal to the Africa Synod:

> We, the priests of the Eastern Deanery of the Archdiocese of Nairobi, in the context of the centenary of the Catholic Church in Kenya (1889–1989), have given extended time in our regular deanery meetings to a pastoral problem that deeply disturbs us: the *Eucharistic famine* of our people. One of us focused on the

> problem in a significant way when he said: "I find myself unable to pray the words of the second Eucharistic prayer: '*May all of us who share in the body and blood of Christ*' . . . while I know the majority of the people present cannot eat at the table of the Lord." This is even more painful because our people are in a large measure also excluded from sharing adequately at the table of the Daily Bread.[1]

This situation is not unique to the Roman Catholic Church. The same issue is found in many Christian denominations in Africa, although not all of them acknowledge it as plainly.

Reasons for the Famine

There are a number of reasons why many of the faithful in Africa are excluded from participation in the Lord's Supper. The first is that many denominations insist that a qualified minister must preside over the ritual. Yet there is a great shortage of presiding ministers. Most Christian congregations in Africa are rural, with the result that a normal parish in most denominations will have several congregations scattered across a vast area and only one minister. In his or her absence, the parish is under the care of trained lay readers or catechists, who are not authorized to preside over the celebration of the Lord's Supper. Roman Catholic canon law stipulates, "The only minister who, in the person of Christ, can bring into being the sacrament of the Eucharist is a validly ordained priest."[2] The Church of the Province of Uganda (presenting the commonly held position of Anglican provinces in Africa) states, "No person shall consecrate and administer the Holy Sacrament of the Lord's Supper unless he/she shall have been Ordained Priest by Episcopal Ordination."[3] The Presbyterian Church of East Africa specifies that "the celebration of Holy Communion is a ministerial act", meaning that only the parish

1. Priests of the Eastern Deanery of the Archdiocese of Nairobi, "Eucharistic Famine: A Pastoral Appeal to the 'Africa Synod'," *African Ecclesiastical Review* (*AFER*) 33, no. 4 (Aug 1991), 178.

2. Canon 900, paragraph 1 in the Roman Catholic *Code of Canon Law*, New revised English translation (Bangalore: Theological Publications in India, 2004), 208.

3. Canon 2.8.1 of the *Provincial Canons of the Church of the Province of Uganda* (Kampala: Centenary Publishing House, 1997), 23.

minister or a member of the presbytery (an ordained minister) can preside.[4] Similarly, the Nigerian Baptist Convention and the Orthodox, Methodist and Lutheran denominations in Africa limit presiding over the Lord's Supper to ordained ministers. A similar practice prevails in many African Instituted Churches (AICs). Even though their practices vary widely and the Lord's Supper is seldom celebrated, when it is, only the founder is regarded as qualified to administer it.[5] There are few protests about this situation because it replicates African culture in which only an elder has the power to bestow blessing.

Another reason why many of the faithful are excluded from the Lord's Supper is the existence of strict church laws regarding marriage. These laws serve to exclude any Christians not married in church from participating in the celebration of the Lord's Supper. For the majority of the denominations mentioned above, only those married in church or those who have had their civil or cultural marriages blessed in church can be admitted to the Lord's Supper. Any other form of marriage is considered invalid. According to Thomas Oduro, Christ Holy Church International in Nigeria excludes the following from the Lord's Supper:

> Polygamists, extra wives of the polygamists, those who are not baptized, those who have not had their marriages blessed, and those who do not attend all of the three-day teaching leading to the Supper.[6]

These and other challenges exclude the majority of believers in Africa from the Lord's Supper and have resulted in a general ignorance of its importance and its benefits, as the following incident shows: A bishop I know was encouraging the youth in his church to consider singing hymns as well as choruses. He also encouraged the celebration of the Lord's Supper at which he wanted some of the hymns to be sung. The young people dismissed the celebration of the Lord's Supper as a complete waste of time compared to singing songs of praise and worship. They

---

4. Section 12:13:2 of the *Practice and Procedure Manual of the Presbyterian Church of East Africa*, 2nd ed. (Nairobi: Publishing Solutions, 1998), 102.

5. Interview with the Venerable John Gichimu, Programme Coordinator for Theology and Ministerial Formation in the Organization of African Instituted Churches (OAIC) at their head office in Nairobi, Kenya, on 25 July 2016.

6. For details see Thomas Oduro, *Christ Holy Church International: The Story of an African Independent Church* (Lagos: Greater Heights Publishers, 2009), 174–175.

were quite sincere when they said this. They simply did not see the value of celebrating the Lord's Supper. Even though many of them had been confirmed in the Christian faith and had participated in the Eucharist, it did not occur to them that it had any bearing on their spiritual well-being and journey of faith. Their church had emphasized only the importance of repentance, being born again, prayer, preaching the word of God, Christian witness and the praise and worship of God. This was the message the church had received from the Church Missionary Society (CMS) missionaries who had brought the Christian faith to the area. They had laid little stress on the Lord's Supper and had introduced a form of faith devoid of rituals.

The same attitude has also affected the way the Lord's Supper is celebrated in many African Instituted Churches. Although there is great diversity among them, it is generally only celebrated at Easter (although the elderly may be given Holy Communion at other times if they request it). In East Africa, Roho churches celebrate an agape meal rather than Holy Communion, whereas Akurinu churches celebrate the Lord's Supper for seven days following the pattern of the children of Israel's commemoration of the Passover. The Zionist and Apostolic churches in Southern Africa celebrate the Lord's Supper following the pattern laid out in the New Testament. Christ's Holy Church International in Nigeria strictly adheres to the name "the Lord's Supper" and always celebrates it in the evenings, arguing that this is required because the sacrament was instituted at night.[7]

Yet despite the fact that the Lord's Supper is often relegated to a secondary position, it remains the central Christian ritual. It celebrates the life, death and resurrection of Jesus Christ – whose death is at the heart of the gospel of salvation, in fulfilment of both the law and the message of the prophets of the Old Testament. How can we then dare to ignore it in our church life?

7. Interview with the Venerable John Gichimu.

Why the Lord's Supper Matters

The majority of congregations in Africa can go on for many weeks, months and even a year without ever participating in the celebration of the Lord's Supper. This is shocking not because the Lord's Supper is a church ritual but because failure to observe it represents blatant disobedience to Jesus Christ's explicit command. At the institution of the Lord's Supper, he told his disciples: "Do this in remembrance of me" (Luke 22:19). He clearly meant that his disciples were to continue to celebrate the Lord's Supper. Thus the Lord's Supper is not an optional extra. It is not something we can leave to chance or celebrate only as the mood takes us. It is mandatory because it is something our Saviour and Lord commanded us to do regularly. Celebration of the Lord's Supper must be an essential part of our Christian way of life.

The Apostle Paul was convinced of this, as we can see in his letter to the believers in Corinth. There he gives the earliest account of the Lord's Supper in the New Testament:

> For I received from the Lord what I also handed on to you, that the Lord Jesus on the night when he was betrayed took a loaf of bread, and when he had given thanks, he broke it and said, "This is my body which is for you. Do this in remembrance of me." In the same way he took the cup also, after supper, saying, "This cup is the new covenant in my blood. Do this, as often as you drink it, in remembrance of me." For as often as you eat this bread and drink the cup, you proclaim the Lord's death until he comes. (1 Cor 11:23–26)

In this passage, Paul gives a second reason why the celebration of the Lord's Supper is something that Christians ought to do as often as possible: in this sacrament we "proclaim the Lord's death until he comes" (1 Cor 11:26). Celebrating the Lord's Supper is one way in which we bear witness to the death and resurrection of our Lord and Saviour Jesus Christ. Thus it is appropriate to speak of the Lord's Supper as part of our Christian witness to each other and to the world.

It does not greatly matter what name we give to this act of worship. In the Bible, it is referred to as Communion (1 Cor 10:16, KJV), the Lord's Supper (1 Cor 11:20), the Lord's Table (1 Cor 10:21) and the

Breaking of Bread (Acts 2:42; see Luke 24:35; 1 Cor 10:16; Acts 2:46; 20:7, 11; 27:35). In many churches it is referred to as the Eucharist (from the Greek word for thanksgiving (see Mark 14:23; Luke 22:17, 19; 1 Cor 11:24).[8] In Greek and Russian Orthodox churches, its celebration is referred to as the Divine Liturgy. In this book, the terms Lord's Supper, Eucharist and Holy Communion are all used to refer to the church's re-enactment and celebration of the same event – the Lord Jesus's Last Supper as described in Matthew, Mark and Luke.

One advantage of referring to this act of worship as the Lord's Supper is that it reminds us of yet another reason why this ritual is important. Just as the unity of any human family is strengthened by regularly eating together, so the church family is strengthened by sharing in this communal meal. Shorter describes it as "the family-building, church-building sacrament *par excellence* which reconciles and unites us to one another in Christ and makes His body grow".[9] It is an affirmation of our unity as believers in Christ. Paul puts it this way,

> The cup of blessing which we bless, is not a sharing in the blood of Christ? The bread that we break, is it not a sharing in the body of Christ? Because there is one bread, we who are many are one body, for we all partake of the one bread. (1 Cor 10:16–17)

In light of Paul's words, it is sad that over the centuries this meal has become a symbol of our divisions rather than of our unity. This book is not the place to address all of the historical and theological controversies that have led to this state of affairs.[10] Here my main concern is with the celebration of the Lord's Supper in the context of Roman Catholic, Protestant and evangelical churches in Africa. My contention is that the Christian church in Africa has long been starved of the benefits of the Lord's Supper and it is now time to change that!

Just as physical food is a basic human need, so the Lord's Supper is basic to the life of a Christian. Those Christians who are not receiving it can rightly be described as deprived and starving.

8. I. H. Marshall, *Last Supper and Lord's Supper* (Carlisle: Paternoster, 1980), 14–16.

9. A. Shorter, "Eucharistic Famine in Africa", *African Ecclesiastical Review* (*AFER*) 27, no. 3 (June 1985): 131.

10. For a brief summary of some issues relating to the history and theology of the Lord's Supper, see the appendix.

So how can we go about addressing this famine and providing Christians with the spiritual food they need? First, we need to address the immediate problem and get food to the starving. That is what I discuss in chapter 2. But my suggestions there are not by any means the whole answer. In Africa, we know well that even when food is delivered to famine-stricken areas, it is sometimes unpalatable to those who receive it. They eat it only because they have nothing else to eat. No matter how healthy the food is, it will never become part of their diet for it comes from an alien culture. This too is something we need to address in relation to the Lord's Supper.

From chapter 3 on, we will be looking closely at our theological understanding of the Lord's Supper, and considering ways in which our celebration of it needs to change if it is to truly minister to the faithful in Africa. My goal is to help us make the Lord's Supper a welcome part of African Christian culture, a ritual that helps African Christians grow to maturity in their understanding of their faith and of their society. In other words, I will seek to respond to the "persistent and growing call for a worship developed in Africa for Africans".[11]

11. Emmanuel C. Anagwo, "Christianity and the African Culture: Integrating the Vision of Liturgical Inculturation", *African Ecclesiastical Review* (*AFER*) 56, no. 4 (2014): 276.

2

IMMEDIATE REMEDIES

In times of famine, two responses are called for. The first addresses the immediate problem and provides food for the starving. The second is more complex, for it involves addressing the factors that led to the famine and changing the situation so that a famine will not occur again. In this chapter, I will deal with the first response to the eucharistic famine by addressing the two main problems identified in the previous chapter as reasons for the famine. While the solutions I suggest may be controversial, they are not complex. If they were instituted, many of the starving would be fed.

Relieving Famine by Providing Officiants

The first reason I identified for the eucharistic famine was the lack of authorized officiants. So let us look at this issue more closely.

The demographic challenge

The demographic landscape of Christianity in Africa is changing. The number of Christians is growing so rapidly that it has outpaced the supply of well-trained African ministers, pastors and theologians.

This problem is not merely because of the time lag between people becoming Christians and their deciding to train for ministry. No, the problem goes much deeper. While the church is growing, there has been a dramatic decrease in the number of students enrolling for courses in theology and ministerial training. The reasons for this include a lack of funds to pay for training, and a lack of paid employment possibilities for pastors.

I can illustrate the result of this shortage from my own experience. In 1995 I was posted to Kogere Parish in Kasese District, Uganda. The headquarters of that parish was just four kilometres from Kasese town, but there were also eight rural congregations scattered over a wide area. I was meant to serve them all. Even if I had visited a different congregation each week, I would have been able to visit each of them only six times a year. Even that low goal was not always achievable, for I inevitably had to spend more time at the main parish church.

The rural congregations were under the care of lay readers who had trained at the diocesan training centre for two years before being commissioned. They were responsible for all aspects of pastoral care and ministry among the believers – except that they could not administer the sacraments of baptism and the Lord's Supper. So the believers in those rural churches could only celebrate the Lord's Supper about twice a year, while those at the main parish celebrated it more regularly.

This state of affairs was by no means unique to that diocese or denomination. It exists in many parts of Africa and across denominations. Millions of African Christians in rural villages away from parish centres are still cared for by leaders who are forbidden to celebrate the Lord's Supper.

What can be done to alleviate the shortage of ministers qualified to celebrate the Lord's Supper? There is no way that current training models for ministers will ever produce enough graduates to meet the need.

Roman Catholics are well aware of this problem and have been debating how to address it. It has even been suggested that, while retaining the seminary model for training priests, the Roman Catholic Church should "experiment with the one which many people have been suggesting for over twenty years: ordain mature married men for as long as a time as the present African situation endures".[1] Revolutionary as such an approach would be, it would not be enough to solve the problem. Even if the church in Africa could somehow have a sufficient number of trained ministers, Christian rural communities would be too poor to pay them any kind of living wage.[2]

1. John C. Ganly, "The Eucharistic Famine in Africa", *African Ecclesiastical Review* (*AFER*) 27, no. 5 (October 1985): 303.

2. Ganly, "Eucharistic Famine", 303.

Lay administration of the Lord's Supper

The endemic famine of the Lord's Supper in Africa, caused largely by the lack of ministers qualified to serve it, will only be adequately addressed when the church on the continent sanctions lay administration of the Lord's Supper. For many people and denominations, the mere mention of this possibility is anathema. I can hear them saying, "This man is out of his mind and should be excommunicated!" They see the prospect of lay people presiding at the Lord's Supper as the thin edge of the wedge, unleashing a torrent of heresy and disaster on the church!

If you are tempted to respond in similar terms, can I urge you to take a deep breath at this point and prayerfully consider what I am going to say in the paragraphs that follow. As you read, ask yourself how the risen Lord Jesus who instituted the Lord's Supper and whose sacrificial death it celebrates would see this issue.

What does the Bible say about lay administration?

As always, the Bible is the place to begin when approaching this issue. Let us go back to our roots and consider prayerfully the available evidence about the way the Lord's Supper (or the breaking of bread) was celebrated in the infant church in Acts. What exactly happened? How was the Lord's Supper celebrated? Who presided? What qualified someone to preside at the Lord's Supper in the early church?

To answer these questions, I looked at all the New Testament references to the Lord's Supper (1 Cor 10:16–17, 21; 1 Cor 11:20–34; Acts 2:42, 46; 20:7, 11; 27:35; Mark 14:17–25; Luke 22:14–23; 24:35; Acts 2:46; 20:7, 11; 27:35). In none of them could I find any mention of the special qualifications and unique responsibility of those serving it.

Given the New Testament's silence on who should administer or preside over the Lord's Supper, I find myself wondering why this ministry has come to be ring-fenced as an exclusive responsibility of priests or presbyters (elders). Of course, it is reasonable to assume that the apostles and other appointed presbyters (elders) did preside over the Lord's Supper. But nowhere in the whole of Scripture is it said to be their exclusive responsibility. Nor does Scripture anywhere state that all others were prohibited from administering the Lord's Supper.

The early Christian community described in the New Testament did not have priests (Greek *hiereus* and Latin *sacerdos*). Only the risen Lord

Jesus Christ was referred to as priest. It was only in the third century that the title "priest" came to be applied to Christian leaders, and only in the fifth and sixth centuries that it became a common term for all Christian ministers.[3] It is reasonable to conclude, therefore, that the church has taken advantage of the silence of Scripture to legislate an absolute prohibition of lay and diaconal administration of the Lord's Supper.

It seems that here we have a particular role being given a prominence that is above (and outside) Scripture. Note that in saying this I am not following the Puritan path and insisting that what is not contained in Scripture is prohibited. Rather, I am asking that we consider the more reasonable point that "what is not contained in Scripture is unessential".[4]

Vincent J. Donovan, a Catholic priest who ministered among the Masai in Kenya, had to think about these issues when the believers confronted him with a similar problem by asking some very pertinent questions:

> What does it mean that we are baptized? Just that, that water was poured on our heads by you? Or does it not mean that we ourselves can now baptize? What does it mean that we are baptized? That we can receive eucharist from your hands any time you chose to come and visit us? Or does it not mean that we are a eucharistic people?[5]

Donovan's response to these questions is telling:

> They were right, certainly. And I had to admit to them that they were right. It was not scripture or theology which prevented them from doing what they thought they had a right to do, but simply the history of a Church imbedded in a single culture, with its own ideas, coming from that culture, as to what number of years of seminary training were needed to lead a community in the simple act of celebrating the Lord's Supper, as he told us to do. Any command of his to undergo academic training

3. Bernard Cooke and Gary Macy, *Christian Symbol and Ritual: An Introduction* (Oxford: Oxford University Press, 2005), 128.

4. R. T. Beckwith and J. E. Tiller, eds., *Holy Communion and its Revision*, Latimer Monographs III (Appleford: Marcham Manor Press, 1972), 39.

5. J. Vincent Donovan, *Christianity Rediscovered: An Epistle from the Masai* (London: SCM, 1978, 1982), 122.

before attempting to break bread together is strictly missing in scripture.[6]

What do churches outside Africa do?

In the process of writing this book, I visited England to research eucharistic celebration and to assess trends in eucharistic celebration in various Christian communities there. I met an Anglican priest who had been in charge of a parish with about three congregations. He obviously could not be at all these congregations every Sunday, and so some of the members of the congregations asked him to allow them to preside over the eucharistic celebration. He was prepared to allow them to do this, provided two conditions were met: First, all the members of the congregation had to be willing to accept this, and second, that the bishop not be told. One of the congregations did fulfil these requirements, and he gave permission for one of the lay members there to preside over the eucharistic celebration. But, he insisted, due process was still important. To maintain order within the church, any layperson wanting to preside over the eucharistic celebration would need to be commissioned to do so.

This issue of lay administration of the Lord's Supper has also been discussed for over thirty years in the Anglican Diocese of Sydney, Australia. The discussions have centred on "whether the absolute prohibition against anyone except the priest (or presbyter) administering the Lord's Supper should continue or be removed for theological reasons".[7] As the authors of a book reporting on these discussions put it, "the Bible is entirely silent on who should administer the Lord's Supper. The conventional Anglican prohibition has no root whatsoever in Scripture".[8]

They argue that the issue needs to be considered first as a theological matter and secondly as a doctrinal one. When this is done, it becomes clear that there are no theological or doctrinal reasons for the absolute prohibition of lay and diaconal administration of the Lord's Supper.[9] The only reason the prohibition exists is that the church has put so much

---

6. Donovan, 122.
7. Peter Bolt, et al., *The Lord's Supper in Human Hands: Who Should Administer?* (Camperdown: Australian Church Record, 2008), 4. See also the *Epilogue* to that volume – Peter Bolt et al., *The Lord's Supper in Human Hands: Epilogue* (Camperdown: Australian Church Record, 2010).
8. Bolt et al., *Lord's Supper in Human Hands*, 5.
9. See Bolt et al., *Lord's Supper in Human Hands*, 22–28, 34, 46 for details.

emphasis on the role of the priest with regard to the celebration of the Lord's Supper. Yet, as I pointed out above, the office of priest was only introduced long after New Testament times.

The reluctance to introduce lay administration of the Lord's Supper is even stranger given that the Anglican Articles of Faith make it clear that the efficacy of the sacrament is independent of the person who administers it. Sacraments are means of God's grace and are appropriated by faith in Jesus Christ who ordained them, regardless of who administers them. Look at Article XXVI: the meaning is clear even if the language is archaic.

> XXVI. Of the Unworthiness of the Ministers, which hinders not the effect of the Sacraments.
>
> Although in the visible Church the evil be ever mingled with the good, and sometimes the evil have chief authority in the Ministration of the Word and Sacraments, yet forasmuch as they do not the same in their own name, but in Christ's, and do minister by his commission and authority, we may use their Ministry, both in hearing the Word of God, and in receiving the Sacraments. Neither is the effect of Christ's ordinance taken away by their wickedness, nor the grace of God's gifts diminished from such as by faith, and rightly, do receive the Sacraments ministered unto them; which be effectual, because of Christ's institution and promise, although they be ministered by evil men.[10]

How will we maintain due order?

If my proposal for lay administration of the Lord's Supper were to be adopted, how would we ensure that due order is maintained? For me, the answer is rooted in African culture.

Elders play a major role in many African communities, and particularly in rural communities. So the elders who are already present in many rural congregations in Africa should be given instruction in matters relating to the Lord's Supper and commissioned to administer it to their congregations. By adopting this approach, we can end the eucharistic

---

10. *Book of Common Prayer*. See further: anglicansonline.org/basics/thirty-nine_articles.html. Accessed 3 March 2016.

famine among God's people that threatens the lived Christian experience of the majority of believers on the African continent.

Such an approach will address the current lack of ministers to administer the Lord's Supper. Careful selection, instruction and commissioning of the lay people to administer the Lord's Supper will also address concerns about order in the administration of the Lord's Supper. I am not suggesting that anybody should be able to administer the Lord's Supper whenever and wherever they choose. Careful selection, instruction and commissioning of the concerned lay people will still be required.

Relieving Famine by Recognizing Marriages

Almost all denominations in Africa draw a strict line between those who have had a church wedding and those who are customarily married. Those who have not had their union blessed in church are forbidden to partake of the Lord's Supper. The priests of the Eastern Deanery of the Archdiocese of Nairobi identified this as the main reason many in their congregations were excluded from the Lord's Supper.[11] The result is that many believers in Africa are "either disfranchised in the eucharistically privileged church or excluded from even a minimum full participation in the infrequent celebrations of the eucharistically underprivileged".[12]

African understandings of marriage

The importance attached to church marriage has had very little impact on African understandings of marriage. In 1980, Archbishop P. Dery of Tamale (Ghana) put it this way, and little has changed in the intervening years:

> Most Catholics feel no need and are often in no hurry for a Church marriage. Customary marriage, in the minds of most Ghanaians, including Catholics, is the *real marriage*. The ceremony in church is seen not as a celebration of marriage but

11. Priests of the Eastern Deanery, "Eucharistic Famine", 179.
12. Shorter, "Eucharistic Famine", 153.

> rather a condition for the reception of the sacraments: a rule of the clergy, a simple blessing, and a foreign import.[13]

One reason for this perception is that a church wedding is a brief matter that is over in a couple of hours, whereas a traditional marriage ceremony involves a lengthy process that may even take years to complete. Moreover, in African societies marriage is a family or clan matter, not merely a contract between two individuals. Ordinarily the entire village community joins in the celebration of a marriage, and "it is not a father or brother or a representative who hands over a bride to the groom, but the whole family or clan to the other family or clan".[14] Archbishop A. Kaseba makes the same point when he says that African customary marriage "is a dynamic whole which creates an alliance . . . And it is *the whole process that makes marriage a reality*".[15]

Archbishop A. Kaseba also insists that "when it comes to the reality of belief and practice of customary marriage, there is no distinction between the faithful in urban areas or cities and those in the rural congregations. Consequently, when Christians do regularize their marriages eventually, very few confess that they had been living in sin".[16] His words are true of the majority of communities in Africa. Those customarily married are in no doubt that theirs is a real marriage. At some point, often at the prompting of church ministers, such couples may come to have their marriages blessed in church so that they can receive the Lord's Supper or be admitted to certain governing committees of the church, but this is in no way an acknowledgement that they believed they were not married.

Western wedding symbols like rings do not carry the same weight of meaning they carry in the West. Nor do Western wedding dresses with their veils and trains. There is already a great richness of cultural costumes and dress at traditional weddings, and the goods exchanged are not rings but cultural gifts like cows, goats or some other object that is valued in that particular culture.

---

13. Priests of the Eastern Deanery, "Eucharistic Famine", 179.

14. G. Elisha Mbonigaba, "The Indigenization of Liturgy" in Thomas J. Talley, ed., *A Kingdom of Priests: Liturgical Formation of the People of God* (Nottingham: Grove, 1988), 47. A more recent version of the same article can be found on pages 20–32 of *Anglican Liturgical Inculturation in Africa: The Kanamai Statement "African Culture and Anglican Liturgy"*, ed. David Gitari (Bramcote, Nottingham: Grove, 1994).

15. Priests of the Eastern Deanery of the Archdiocese of Nairobi, "Eucharistic Famine", 179.

16. Priests of the Eastern Deanery, "Eucharistic Famine", 179.

In East Africa, churches have begun to conduct mass weddings to encourage those in customary marriages to have their marriages regularized in church. As many as two hundred couples may be married at a single event – often only after a lengthy campaign spearheaded by the ministers. While such efforts are to be commended, they are not the long-term solution to the problem of those in customary marriages being excluded from the Lord's Supper.

> [They] do not go to the root of the pastoral problem. This is the failure of effective dialogue between the Church's law and the socio-cultural realities of African customary marriage and family life. Until such a dialogue is effective, church marriage will remain the priest's exclusive concern. It also means that large numbers of people will be deprived of communion for very long periods, assisting, often assiduously, at a meal where the food is denied them.[17]

Even as these campaigns and mass wedding ceremonies are being held, customary marriages continue to be contracted. Remember, the majority of those contracting customary marriages may not even be aware of the benefits of the Lord's Supper for their spiritual growth.[18] Moreover, it seems to me that in its insistence on church weddings, the church itself is lagging behind what is happening among the people. There have been, and continue to be, many changes in regard to traditional wedding customs, so that it is no longer possible to draw a clear line between a traditional ceremony and a church ceremony.

Customary marriage and church marriage

I recently had the opportunity to attend a traditional marriage ceremony where I was asked to give a word of exhortation. Among the Banyankole and Bakiga of Western and South Western Uganda, the traditional ceremony is called *kuhingira*. It is an elaborate, public ceremony in which the father of the girl officially hands his daughter over to the parents of the boy in the presence of the boy and relatives and friends from both families. I must confess that after attending this ceremony,

17. Shorter, "Eucharistic Famine", 135.
18. Shorter, 136.

I was left wondering what was left to do in church the next day. To all intents and purposes, the *kuhingira* ceremony is a complete wedding ceremony blessed by God.

Before you rush to judge me for saying this, let me sketch for you what generally happens at a *kuhingira* ceremony. Note that the description I am about to give applies not only to the cultural marriage ceremony I attended but is also what happens at cultural marriage ceremonies in the majority of communities in Uganda.

The ceremony begins with relatives and friends of the two families gathering in the home of the parents of the girl to celebrate the joy of this alliance. As is typical of African spirituality and hospitality, there is eating, singing and dancing. The boy (the bridegroom) is introduced by the girl to her parents, who then receive him as a member of their family. Later the girl (the bride), wearing a traditionally designed dress, is introduced by the bridegroom to his parents, who in turn joyfully welcome her into their family. These introductions are followed by speeches from both sides and an exchange of traditional gifts. Then an invited minister is asked to give a word of exhortation from the Bible.

The ceremony reaches its climax when representatives of both families are asked to move to the centre (the ceremony takes place in an open compound, in full view of all who are present). The parents of the boy stand with their son and relatives on one side. The parents of the girl stand with their daughter and relatives on the other side. The ministers present are asked to come to the centre. The father of the girl officially and physically hands over the girl to the parents of the boy, amidst shouts of joy and thanksgiving. Then one of the senior ministers is asked to say a prayer and pronounce a blessing.

I hope you can now appreciate my dilemma. In my view, such a ceremony is a complete marriage at which God is present. But church law requires that there be another function in church the next day (or some other day) for a Western-style wedding with white gowns and everything else associated with the Western idea of marriage. This imposes additional expenses that deter many poor Christians from even considering a church marriage.

When we insist on doing things in a Western way, what are we saying about our own values and customs? Are we saying that they are inferior to European values and customs?

We all need to acknowledge that where a customary or traditional marriage has taken place, "the Christian ceremony has little meaning for most Africans, and the traditional wedding rites do not necessarily support a Christian understanding of marriage".[19]

Given this situation, there can be little doubt that the church's regulations on marriage need to be brought into dialogue with the reality of African customary marriage with a view of recognising customary marriages.

I am pleased to hear that in Nigeria the church is making efforts to respond to the people's need for a culturally meaningful marriage celebration. There the *Igba Nkwu* (the culminating ceremony in a traditional marriage) and a church wedding are combined on the same day at the same venue (usually the home of the bride).[20] This may not be a perfect example, but is an appropriate response and step in the right direction.

Cardinal J. A. Malula, speaking in Yaounde in 1982, had this to say to his audience:

> Certainly it is of divine faith that Christ has affirmed and taught the indissolubility of marriage. In Africa we know it and teach it also. But we believe also that Christ did not say how people of different cultures should marry, nor when the marriage validly contracted becomes absolutely indissoluble. For this reason only the affirmation of the indissolubility should be considered a divine law and absolute command. The matter of contracting a marriage (e.g. canonical form) and the conditions of its indissolubility (e.g. consummation with one single sexual act), are they revealed by God? Are they not cultural phenomena in time and space?[21]

It is worth noting that most of the church laws regulating marriage arose in sixteenth-century Europe to deal with issues arising from the secret marriages that were being contracted at that time. But marriage

19. Aylward Shorter, "Liturgical Creativity in Africa", *African Ecclesiastical Review* (*AFER*) 5 (1977): 266.
20. Patrick C. Chibuko, "A Practical Approach to Liturgical Inculturation", *African Ecclesiastical Review* (*AFER*) 43, no. 1–2 (2001): 7.
21. Priests of the Eastern Deanery of The Archdiocese of Nairobi, "Eucharistic Famine", 182.

in Africa has always been a public event, contracted in the full view of relatives, friends and neighbours. So what we have now is a case where church regulations designed to address specific issues in a specific context are being transplanted and imposed on African communities in a completely different context. Sadly, they have come to be regarded as part of the gospel message.

In advocating for the recognition of traditional marriages, I am not in any way advocating for a blanket admission of all to the Lord's Supper. Paul exhorts us to examine ourselves first before we partake (1 Cor 11:27–33). One cannot disregard the consequences of approaching the Lord's Table in an unworthy manner.

I am also well aware of the moral breakdown in African communities that has resulted in many ungodly practices, including casual unions, promiscuity and prostitution. This kind of moral breakdown is not confined to Africa. Sin does corrupt what God created as a good gift to humanity and uses it to dehumanize, degrade and cause untold pain. That is why the transforming power of the gospel needs to be shared with all so they can attain the salvation that comes by grace through faith in Jesus Christ.

To sum up, church marriage legislation and the discipline that flows from it need to be re-examined in respect of legally contracted, monogamous, customary African marriages. The absolute exclusion of those customarily married from the Lord's Supper is a cause of malnourishment to many who may not even be aware of what they lack. This type of famine among God's people can no longer be defended or justified. A dialogue between the marriage law and the reality of customary marriages in various socio-cultural groups in Africa remains the only long-term solution to the exclusion of many from the Lord's Supper.

3

AFRICAN CULTURES AND CHRISTIAN TRADITION

In the previous chapters, I addressed two of the major reasons why Christians in Africa are not being nourished by the Lord's Supper. But we cannot solve this problem merely by changing church laws. We need to work towards a way of understanding and celebrating the Lord's Supper that will contribute to an African's understanding of the meaning and significance of the death of Christ for the faithful.

The above paragraph also serves to highlight one of the problems I face when talking about how to celebrate the Lord's Supper in a way that resonates with African thinking. What is "African"? How do we distinguish between what is African and what is not? Given that culture is constantly changing, what does the term "African" refer to? Does it refer to the culture of the last century, or the one before that? Does it refer to rural culture or to contemporary African culture in cities like Lagos, Nairobi, Abidjan and Johannesburg, with all their diversity? How do we define ourselves as Africans?

There are some who argue that we should go back to our roots to find a fitting definition of what is African. I suppose by this they mean we should go back to pre-colonial days and find our identity there. But defining what is African through the lenses of pre-colonial Africa implies that "Africans are increasingly less African, and African culture becomes a museum piece".[1] The approach that focuses on the past misses the point that culture is dynamic and not static.

1. Klaus Fiedler, *Christianity and African Culture: Conservative German Protestant Missionaries*

In this book, the definition that I have adopted is that "African is what is relevant for Africans".[2] That which is African is both acceptable and relevant to African peoples – it is of value and for the good of the people of Africa. Like all other societies, African societies exercise discernment, retaining or rejecting some of their old values and integrating new values that arise internally or from contact with other cultures, all this while remaining fully African. This also applies in regard to the way they participate in rituals such as the Lord's Supper.

It is also important to stress that Africa is not one homogenous society. Some Westerners think they know Africa when they have visited only one part of Africa. Someone who hears that I come from Uganda may ask me questions about Nigeria, which is thousands of miles away from Uganda, with a population and geographical area that are over five times that of Uganda. What this diversity means in practice is that the examples shared in this and subsequent chapters are drawn from particular African societies, and while they may point to what we are likely to find in other African societies, I am not going to claim that they are representative per se. Each African culture is a unique whole.

While this book is not the place for a comprehensive treatise on what constitutes culture and how it is maintained and perpetuated, it may be useful to pause to reflect on these issues before moving on to discuss the relationship between the Christian tradition and culture in general.[3] An understanding of these issues will help us in our attempts to promote the meaningful celebration of the Christian sacrament of the Lord's Supper in Africa.

---

in Tanzania 1900–1940 (Leiden: Brill, 1996), 165.

2. Fiedler, 165.

3. For detailed surveys of culture and how it relates to the Christian tradition, see the classic works of Richard H. Niebuhr, *Christ and Culture* (London: Faber & Faber, 1952); D. A. Carson, *Christ and Culture Revisited* (Grand Rapids, MI: Eerdmans, 2008); Charles H. Kraft. *Christianity in Culture: A Study in Dynamic Biblical Theologizing in Cross-Cultural Perspective* (Maryknoll, NY: Orbis, 1979).

What Is Culture?

When we speak of culture, we are referring to "the total process of human activity and that total result of such activity . . . It comprises language, habits, ideas, beliefs, customs, social organization, inherited artifacts, technical processes, and values".[4] Another definition states that culture is

> the sum total of all people's traditional religions, customs, traditions, rites, ceremonies, symbols, art, wisdom and institutions . . . It is based on a people's world view, the way they relate to the Supreme Being, to the supernatural powers and phenomena, to their fellow men and women, to the world of other living beings and inanimate beings, and to the world underground.[5]

By this broad definition, culture includes my traditional spiritual environment; what I wear; what food I eat and how I prepare and eat that food; the songs I sing; the musical instruments I use; my name; how I celebrate birth, marriage and death; and even my language. In fact, although culture includes language, culture itself is a kind of language – our particular cultures tell something about our identity, that is, about who we are. And the rituals and gestures we use in our cultures convey meanings that are best understood by those who share the same culture.

There is thus no such thing as an uncultured people. We may not like or approve of the way other people conduct themselves or the food they eat, but that is their culture, and it is probably different from our own. Sometimes, these differences can be surprising and even shocking. Consider the following encounter between a missionary in Northern Congo and local elders:

> "We are not going to have our wives dress like prostitutes," protested an elder in the Ngbaka Church in Northern Congo, as he replied to the suggestion made by the missionary that the women should be required to wear blouses to cover their breasts. The Church leaders were unanimous in objecting to

4. Niebuhr, *Christ and Culture*, 32, 46.
5. John Mary Waliggo, Arij Roest Crollius, T. Nkeramihigo, and J. Mutiso-Mbinda, *Inculturation: Its Meaning and Urgency* (Nairobi: St. Paul Publications, 1986), 27.

> such requirement, for in that part of Congo the well-dressed and fully dressed African women were too often prostitutes, since they alone had money to spend on attractive garments.[6]

So we have cultural differences in our opinions about the amount of clothing one should put on to be considered decently dressed. This point has even been brought home to me in the context of the Lord's Supper: I will never forget seeing "altar girls" clad in traditional Zulu attire serving at the holy table at a confirmation service in a church in Pietermaritzburg in South Africa. No one besides my colleagues from Nigeria and I appeared at all bothered by their almost bare chests and extremely short skirts.

It is not surprising that culture affects what we wear in church and how we conduct ourselves in church, because a church community is part of a society, and "social life is always cultural . . . culture and social existence go together".[7] It is our culture that teaches us what we should or should not do in specific situations. This is why any attempt to introduce a new way of doing things or some new behaviour in a society will inevitably be met with resistance, as many missionaries to Africa can testify. Similar resistance can be expected by those who attempt to make any change in regard to the way the Lord's Supper is observed and celebrated.

Opposition to change is particularly strong because values are a key part of culture. In fact, Don Edwards defined culture as having to do with the "meanings, values, and patterns of a social group; a code which makes a social group understandable; and that through which we learn the meaning of the world".[8] That is why all cultures have strong systems in place to ensure that these "meanings, values, and patterns" are passed on to the next generation. They are a key element in the group's identity.

But while cultural change will always be resisted, it is also pervasive, for culture is dynamic. Culture is not static; it is living.

> The cultural patterning that we pass on to the next generation, though it retains an extremely high degree of similarity to

---

6. Eugene A. Nida, *Customs and Cultures: Anthropology for Christian Missions* (New York: Harper & Brothers, 1954), 1.

7. Niebuhr, Christ and Culture, 47.

8. Don Edwards, "Christ and Culture: Some Preliminary Reflections", *Colloquium* 28, no. 2 (1996): 84.

> the patterning that we receive is never exactly the same. . . . Whether under duress or not, each person and group constantly alters the cultural patterns they have received, usually in fairly minor ways, and passes on to those of the next generation a slightly differing set of patterns than those received. In this way every culture is constantly having its patterning altered. Thus the cultural patterning altered by generation I becomes the received patterning of generation II, that altered by generation II becomes the received patterning of generation III etc.[9]

Every cultural group everywhere on the globe experiences change, which sometimes comes from within and sometimes from external influence from other cultural communities. In our increasingly globalized world, modern technology and increased population mobility have made it a lot easier for different communities to interact and influence each other. But just as a person retains their unique identity while going through all the changes in their life cycle, "so culture retains a certain homogeneity through all its changes unless it is violently altered, for example, through conquest or exile".[10] The people of some of the great monarchies in Africa, for example, the Zulu in South Africa, the Sotho of Lesotho and the Baganda of Uganda, have experienced great changes in their way of life. Their cultural institutions are certainly not those of the eighteenth century. Yet amidst all the noticeable changes, these monarchies and their peoples have remained identifiable as distinct cultural groups in the twenty-first century. Similarly, the way in which we celebrate the Lord's Supper has changed over the centuries and in different cultures, and yet it still retains clear links to its New Testament origins.

Relationship between God and Culture

But is this reality of cultural adaptation a good or a bad thing? Should we be adapting our celebration of the Lord's Supper to different cultures, or should we be aiming to get back to the New Testament culture in which

---

9. Charles H. Kraft, *Christianity in Culture* (Maryknoll, NY: Orbis, 1979), 70–71.

10. James Chukwuma Okoye, "Eucharist in African Perspective", *Mission Studies* 19, no. 1–2 (2002): 161.

the ritual originated, or to the centuries old tradition of the Western church? Or should we be aiming to root our celebration of the Lord's Supper in our African cultures? Answering these questions requires an understanding of the relationship between God and culture. How does Christ relate to the various cultures of the various socio-cultural groups in Africa? This question becomes even more pertinent when we recognize that it includes aspects of African culture that missionaries considered superstitious. What is God's attitude to them? This question and many other related questions need to be honestly addressed if Christianity is to be fully inculturated among African peoples.

Over the centuries, Christian thinkers have adopted four positions with regard to the relationship between God and culture. These can be identified as "God-against-culture, God-in-culture, God-above-culture and God-above-but-through culture".[11]

God-against-culture

There are some who regard African culture as evil, and therefore as something that is outside the realm of God. People who hold this view will strongly reject any attempt to introduce any African elements into our celebration of the Lord's Supper.

This view that God is opposed to culture has ancient roots, beginning with the hatred some early Christians felt towards Jewish culture. Later, following the persecution of Christians by the Romans, there was an equal hatred for Greco-Roman culture. This hatred led the authors of some second-century writings such as *The Teaching of the Twelve, The Shepherd of Hermas, The Epistle of Barnabas* and *The First Epistle of Barnabas*, to "present Christianity as a way of life quite separate from culture". These writers argue that "Christians constitute a new people, a third race besides Jews and Gentiles".[12]

Those who like these ancient writers espouse the God-against-culture position argue that "God is opposed to culture; the choice for

11. Kraft, *Christianity in Culture*, 104–115. Kraft acknowledges his indebtedness to Niebuhr's *Christ and Culture*, in which Niebuhr addressed the relationship between Christ and culture under the following subheadings: Christ against Culture, The Christ of Culture, Christ above Culture, Christ and Culture in Paradox, and Christ the Transformer of Culture. In *Christ and Culture Revisited*, D. A. Carson has reviewed the work of H. Richard Niebuhr and provided a helpful critique.

12. Niebuhr, *Christ and Culture*, 62.

commitment to God is by definition a decision to oppose culture".[13] Here culture is equated to the world that is under the power of the evil one. Culture is therefore an evil that surrounds believers, who ought to be careful to separate themselves from it. The way to holiness "is to escape from and to condemn the world".[14] It was this type of thinking that contributed to the growth of monastic orders in which believers could live in physical separation from the evil around them.[15]

Tertullian, a great North African theologian, seems to have been the most outspoken proponent of the Christ-against-culture position. He insisted that there was no positive relationship between culture and Christianity and sharply rejected any claims to anything good in culture for a Christian, maintaining that

> the conflict of the believer is not with nature but culture, for it is in culture that sin chiefly resides. Tertullian comes very close to the thought that original sin is transmitted through society, and that if it were not for the vicious customs that surround a child from its birth and for its artificial training its soul would remain good.[16]

For many proponents of this view, the solution to maintaining purity as a Christian lies in separation – believers must separate themselves from culture. Consequently "the recommendation for Christians is to withdraw, reject, escape, isolate, and insulate themselves from the world in order to develop and maintain holiness".[17]

The Christ-against-culture position is rooted in the fallacy that culture is an external reality. But in truth culture is both an internal and external reality. We can never separate ourselves from it or escape from it, for wherever we go, we carry it with us.[18] While it is possible to "innovate, replace, add to, transform, and in other ways alter our use of the culture

---

13. Kraft, *Christianity in Culture*, 104.
14. Kraft, 104. Proponents of this position find support in passages like 1 John 2:15–16 and 5:19 that warn believers against loving the world.
15. Kraft, 105.
16. Niebuhr, *Christ and Culture*, 65.
17. Kraft, *Christianity in Culture*, 105.
18. Kraft, 105–106.

that we have received",[19] it is impossible to escape from culture. To put it differently, "Culture is not a reality on the ground: it is in the mind".[20]

To attempt to separate yourself from your culture so you can flee from it is to set yourself an impossible task. If I may put it this way, how can one flee from oneself? Your culture is your identity. Your culture has made you what you are in totality. We cease to be human beings outside the realm of culture. Besides, there is no Christianity that is not culturally conditioned, for "all forms of Christianity are inherently and unavoidably embedded in cultural practices".[21]

As the Tanzanian scholar Laurenti Magesa remind us,

> "Christianity" is an expression of convenience; it is always a cultural reality. Whenever we use the term we must, therefore try to be conscious of the fact that we are referring to a particular appearance of Christianity, a contextualized fact. Strictly speaking there is no universal Christianity, only various specific, culturally and linguistically-conditioned manifestations of our faith in Christ (Acts 11:26) . . . So, if we have to speak about "Christianity" we must bear in mind its situated or context-defined specifically rather than its universal sense.[22]

God-in-culture

At the opposite extreme from the God-against-culture view is an equally distorted and extreme position on God's attitude to culture: the God-in-culture position. Proponents of this view, "believe that, one way or another, God is contained either within culture in general or within one specific culture".[23]

We need to distinguish between two God-in-culture positions. The first argues that God (or Christ) is in culture in the sense that God is no more than a cultural construct. It is said that different societies have developed different understandings of God "wholly or largely as the

---

19. Kraft, 106.

20. Okoye, "Eucharist in African Perspective", 160.

21. Carson, *Christ and Culture Revisited*, 3.

22. Laurenti Magesa, unpublished paper, "Theological Dialogue between the Christian Faith and African Culture", presented to the Council of Anglican Provinces in Africa (CAPA), Theological Consultation, on Wednesday, September 3, 2014, p. 3.

23. Kraft, *Christianity in Culture*, 106.

result of the human quest for suprahuman sanction for the kind of life that a person's culture prescribes". The premise is that "members of different cultures perceive deity in quite different ways" and that "the differences in these perceptions correlate with the differences between the worldviews of these societies".[24] In other words, people, and even Christians, are said to have created God in their own image, and so God is merely a reflection of the culture of those who worship him.

The second position as regards God-in-culture sees "God as contained within, or at least as endorsing, one particular culture". He is seen as "either creating, gradually developing, or endorsing a given culture or subculture, and ordaining that all people everywhere if they are to be Christian be converted thereto".[25] The end result is that one culture comes to be seen as the superior and authorized vehicle of the Christian faith, and almost comes to be understood as the Christian or biblical culture. The theological, ethical, religious beliefs and practices of that culture then become the standard that other cultures should adopt.

This was the belief held by many Jews in New Testament times. They insisted that Yahweh was the God of the Jews and that the only way to relate to him was by adopting Jewish culture. Thus they expected Gentile converts to Christianity to adopt Jewish practices such as circumcision and observe Jewish dietary laws. It took a vision to change Peter's thinking on these issues, and it took Paul's arguments at the Council of Jerusalem (see Acts 15) to persuade the leaders of the church that God accepted Gentile Christians without asking them to live like Jews. Paul sets out his thinking on this topic in Galatians 2.

In recent centuries, we see a variant of this attitude when people claim that the culture of their denomination is superior to that of all other denominations. Sadly, we have also seen it at work when missionaries have assumed that Western culture is superior to African culture. In Uganda, for example, both Protestant and Roman Catholic missionaries denounced the culture of the Baganda as evil, and declared that those who came to Christ had to turn their backs on it. Converts were expected to renounce their Kiganda names and take what became known as "Christian names" – or in other words, English or Italian

---

24. Kraft, 107.
25. Kraft, 107.

names. So you still find Catholic Ugandans being baptized with names like Expeditus or Expedito, while Protestant children receive names like John Watson, Williamson, Wilberforce, and Rose Mary. The extent to which such thinking has penetrated our culture came home to me when I had to convince my own children that they had been duly baptized even though they did not have an English name. The school authorities demanded to see the baptism cards for Mwesigwa ("God is faithful"), Alinda ("God is our keeper", taken from Psalm 121) and Ahebwa ("God our provider"). We had to explain the meaning of baptism so that our children understood that baptism has nothing to do with acquiring an English name. That is the type of confusion that results when we associate God too closely with a culture.

The "God-in-culture" position strongly influences those who insist that the Mediterranean culture in which Jesus Christ instituted the Lord's Supper is normative for its celebration anywhere and everywhere. They insist that churches must use only the Mediterranean food and drink Jesus used. However, as I will be arguing, this attitude reduces the celebration of the Eucharist to a celebration of the Mediterranean diet and not of the risen Lord Jesus Christ who incarnates in all cultures.

God-above-culture

The third view that seeks to define God's attitude to culture is what has been called "God-above-culture". It argues that God is above and outside culture and is not particularly concerned with human affairs.[26] Some of those who adopt this position do acknowledge God as the creator of the world and of people, but they insist that he is no longer in control of day-to-day life – creation is uncontrollably driving itself. God is portrayed as "virtually unreachable in his concern or inability; it is useless for us to waste time calling on him".[27] This is the view of many African communities. They think of God as far removed from the people and unable to control the evil powers that torment them. For example, during the difficult times when the brutal President Idi Amin ruled Uganda (1971–1979), many people believed that the "record files" of Uganda had got misplaced and were no longer in the presence of God. By this,

26. Kraft, 108.
27. Kraft, 109.

they meant that God was no longer in touch with what was happening in Uganda. He was inaccessible and no longer concerned about Ugandan affairs. This feeling became even more intense after Amin brutally killed Archbishop Janani Luwum, who had openly confronted him and spoken out against the extra-judicial killing of Ugandans.[28] Some Christians began arguing that it was a waste of time to say the prescribed prayer for the state and its president. It took the counsel of church leaders to correct this attitude. They encouraged Christians to intensify their prayers for both the nation and its president in those difficult times.

When we are in deep distress, it is all too easy to begin to think that God is out of reach and unconcerned about our affairs. That is when God-above-culture believers start to focus more and more on themselves and deny any sense of need for external help. This in turn leads to humanism and either "denial of the existence of God, denial of our ability to know whether or not he exists or depersonalization of God into some sort of Eternal Principle".[29] This view considers worship, dependence on God, and celebration of the Lord's Supper as meaningless and a waste of time. It argues that people should be encouraged to spend their energy on other activities that improve the human condition.

God-above-but-through-culture

The final position, which is the one I endorse, acknowledges "God as above culture but as using culture as the vehicle for interaction with humans".[30] We see evidence of what this means in practice when we read 1 Corinthians 9:19–22:

> For though I am free with respect to all, I have made myself a slave to all, so that I might win more of them. To the Jews I became as a Jew, in order to win Jews. To those under the law, I became as one under the law (though I myself am not under the law) so that I might win those under the law. To those

28. Archbishop Janani Luwum, the sitting Archbishop of the Anglican Church of Uganda, met his death on 16 February 1977 at the very bloody hands of Idi Amin Dada. Archbishop Luwum is recognized by the Anglican Communion as a twentieth-century martyr, and his statue stands with those of other twentieth-century martyrs in front of Westminster Abbey in London. Uganda now has a national public holiday on 16 February each year to celebrate his life.

29. Kraft, *Christianity in Culture*, 109.

30. Kraft, 113.

> outside the law I became as one outside the law (though I am not free from God's law but I am under Christ's law) so that I might win those outside the law. To the weak I became weak, so that I might win the weak. I have become all things to all people, so that I might by any means save some.

Based on this passage, it is reasonable to suggest that "God views human culture primarily as a vehicle to be used by him and his people for Christian purposes, rather than as an enemy to be combated or shunned".[31]

Given that human beings are by nature sinful, we cannot deny that cultural forms, patterns and processes are tainted with sin: "no aspect of culture is used by human beings with pure intent". But the good news is that "human beings are redeemable"[32] and that culture is not static but dynamic. The human beings who live within a culture are constantly changing and hence influencing the cultural patterns and processes of their society. Sometimes the change in cultural patterns and process is so significant that it can be labelled a "transformation":

> when such transformation takes place as a result of a relationship with God we may speak of the influence of God on culture change. This model assumes that, though God exists totally outside of culture while humans exist totally within culture, God chooses the cultural milieu in which humans are immersed as the arena of his interaction with his people.[33]

Each culture has its own strengths and weaknesses. Yet despite these weaknesses or imperfections, the Bible indicates that when the Sovereign Lord (Yahweh the Creator of the universe, the one who is eternally holy – Lev 19:2; 20:26; 1 Pet 1:15–16) chose to speak to Abraham and Moses, he spoke to them in the language of their culture. He did not use some "new" language they needed to learn first. For example, it is recorded that "the Lord appeared to Abraham by the oaks of Mamre, as he sat at the entrance of his tent in the heat of the day" (Gen 18:1). Abraham then served his heavenly guests culturally appropriate food. They did not

---

31. Kraft, 103.
32. Kraft, 114.
33. Kraft, 114.

come with prepacked "heavenly" meals. They were served bread made from local flour, a calf from Abraham's herd, and milk from his herd (Gen 18:6–8). This food was part of Abraham's culture. It was within this culture that the Lord interacted with Abraham and his wife Sarah.

Even more significantly, when God chose to reveal himself fully, he did it through human culture. This is the story of the "Word" became "flesh" (John 1:14) – the story of the incarnation. As Paul says, "when the fullness of time had come, God sent his Son, born of woman, born under the law" (Gal 3:4). Being "born of woman" points to Jesus being the son of a human mother, and "under the law" points to his Jewishness. God used the human culture of the Jews when he made his final and complete revelation of himself through his Son (Heb 1:1–4). There is no denying that culturally, Jesus was Jewish. Despite the cultural imperfections of the Jewish people, it was through their culture that God chose to reveal himself to his people.

In the same way, God can reveal himself to African people through the Lord's Supper when the life, death and resurrection of the Lord Jesus are celebrated in a way that is relevant and meaningful to Africans. True, God is above culture, but the evidence of the Scriptures is that God interacts with people through their cultures.

Conclusion

Human beings were not created to live alone. We were created with a need for community, and community implies the existence of a culture. It has been proved over and over again that "human beings do not seem to function well in the absence of clearly defined and consistent guidelines for behaviour".[34]

Of culture, it has been said that,

> Culture is not in and of itself either an enemy or friend to God or humans. It is, rather, something that is there to be used by personal beings such as humans, God, and Satan. Culture is the milieu in which all encounters with or between human beings

34. Kraft, 104.

> take place and in terms of which all human understanding and maturation occur.[35]

While I agree with this overall argument, it is inaccurate to speak of culture as an entity apart from the people of that culture. We should not think of culture as something in which human beings are entangled and from which we can be disentangled. Culture is an essential part of our humanity. We are not human beings apart from culture.

The other point that is repeatedly made in this book is that culture is not static. Redeemed human beings begin to act differently, and they begin to use their cultural forms, patterns and processes differently. To give another example, think of how Christian Africans now use drums. In the past, drums were associated with practices in which Christians did not participate. But Africans did not abandon their drums. Today drumming is central to the African musical expression in which we worship a new Master, the Lord Jesus Christ.

What all this means is that "the Church's proclamation must be made in such a way that the Gospel message finds meaningful expression in people's lives and cultures; and this is the way of inculturation".[36] This is what we will be looking at in the next chapter.

35. Kraft, 113.

36. Justin Ukpong, "Inculturation and Evangelization: Biblical Foundations for Inculturation", in Joseph Brookman-Amissah et al., eds., *Inculturation and Mission of the Church in Nigeria* (Port Harcourt: CIWA Press, 1992), 16.

4

INCULTURATION

Inculturation" refers to the way in which "the Christian message transforms culture" while at the same time "Christianity is transformed by culture, not in a way that falsifies the message, but in the way in which the message is formulated and interpreted anew".[1] This sounds very technical, and so you may be surprised and humbled, as I was, to discover that the experts in inculturation are often those who are already living it out in their village churches and homes.

Let me give you an example of how this works in terms of the Christian ritual known as passing the peace: The Masai in Kenya and Tanzania are cattle-herders, and grass is of great significance to them because their cattle graze on it. It has come to symbolize the source of their livelihood and is "a vital and holy sign to them, a sign of peace and happiness and well-being".[2] When there was a dispute or argument in the community, one party would offer the other a tuft of grass to signal their desire for peace rather than conflict. By accepting this tuft, the other party signalled that they agree that there should be peace. This ritual was understood by all in the community. So before each celebration of the Lord's Supper, Vincent J. Donovan, a missionary working among the Masai, would pick a tuft of grass, hand it to the first elder who met him, and say "the peace of Christ". The elder would receive the grass and pass it on to his

1. Aylward Shorter, *Toward a Theology of Inculturation* (London: Geoffrey Chapman, 1988), 13–14. In this work, Shorter helpfully distinguishes between enculturation ("the cultural learning process of the individual, the process by which a person is inserted into his or her culture"), acculturation ("the encounter between one culture and another") and interculturation ("a partnership in mission or evangelism that mutually benefits both the recipient culture and the gospel being preached"). The latter is the most closely related to inculturation.

2. Donovan, *Christianity Rediscovered*, 124–125.

family, who would then pass it on to other elders and their families, who would pass it on to their neighbours, until that tuft of grass had been passed to everyone in the community. It symbolized the brotherhood of all in the community. If for some reason someone or some group in the village "refused to accept the grass as the sign of the peace of Christ, there would be no eucharist at this time".[3]

That example helps us to understand the definition of inculturation "as the process of interpreting and living Christianity (that is, Christian faith and practice) from within the perspective of a particular culture and the people's social and historical life experience in such a way that Christian values are made to animate the people's way of life".[4] It affects not only religious aspects of culture but is holistic in that the interaction between Christianity and culture affects both the religious and secular realms.[5]

Options for Inculturation

But how are we to go about doing inculturation, and doing it in relation to the Lord's Supper? The theologians who have discussed this concept suggest two possible approaches: adaptation and incarnation.[6]

Inculturation as adaptation

To adapt something means to make it fit. For example, people who travel internationally need to carry adapters so that they can plug their computers or phone chargers into the different shapes of the wall sockets in different countries. If they do not have an adapter, they cannot access the local electricity supply. Similarly, in theological terms adaptation refers to a "creative method of pastoral activity, by which we try to adopt the message we share and the liturgy we celebrate to the customs of those we work among".[7]

---

3. Donovan, 127.
4. Justin S. Ukpong, "Inculturation and Evangelization", 10.
5. Justin S. Ukpong, "Inculturation: A Major Challenge to the Church in Africa Today", *African Ecclesiastical Review* (*AFER*) 38, no. 5 (1996): 1.
6. Theologians who have discussed this issue include John Mary Waliggo, Peter Schineller, Phillip Tovey, and L. Magesa.
7. Peter Schineller, *A Handbook on Inculturation* (New York: Paulist, 1990), 16.

But the above definition of adaptation also reveals one of the major problems with this approach. In terms of the computer or phone metaphor, we are changing only the plug but not modifying the equipment to suit the new environment. So the computer or phone may now have power, but without a local SIM card, it will function poorly and may lack access to local data. Similarly, the adaptation model tended to make only superficial changes and to address peripheral issues because it assumed that the message and the liturgy (the SIM card in the metaphor) were already in place. Thus adaptation came to mean no more than "translation of the Latin texts into various African languages, use of African names for God without grappling with traditional religious ideas; accommodating the externals of African life (colour, music, musical instruments) without coming to terms with the fundamental spirit generative of these externals, etc."[8]

Thus adaptation "did not go far enough to express the reality of an indissoluble marriage between Christianity and each local culture".[9] Even the ritual of passing of grass that we mentioned at the start of this chapter can be seen as simply part of an adaptation approach that "implied a selection of certain rites and customs, purifying them and inserting them within Christian rituals where there was any apparent similarity".[10]

Thus it was soon recognized that the "the concept of 'adaptation' contained within itself the seeds of perpetual Western superiority and domination".[11] It ignored pertinent issues of African religious experience and practice and the fact that identifying and isolating unchangeable aspects of the gospel has proved a near impossible task in the history and life of the church of Christ. There is no one brand of "Christianity" that can be called universal. Christianity is always a cultural reality. The discussion on the elements used in celebration of the Lord's Supper in chapter 7 of this book explains this matter further.

8. E. Uzukwu, *Liturgy: Truly Christian, Truly African* (Eldoret, Kenya: Gaba Publications, 1982), 30. For more on the history of liturgical adaptation and the "Magna Carta of Liturgical Adaptation" see Anscar J. Chupungco, *Cultural Adaptation of the Liturgy* (New York: Paulist, 1982), 3–57.

9. Waliggo et al., *Inculturation*, 11.

10. Waliggo et al., 11.

11. Schineller, *Handbook on Inculturation*, 17.

In 1974 at the International Conference on Evangelization in Rome, the bishops from Africa and Madagascar took a clear stand against the adaptation model:

> Our theological thinking must remain faithful to the authentic tradition of the Church and, at the same time, be attentive to the life of our communities and respectful of our traditions and languages, that is of our philosophy of life . . . The Bishops of Africa and Madagascar consider as being completely out-of-date, the so called theology of adaptation. In its stead, they adopt the theology of incarnation. The young churches of Africa cannot refuse to face up to this basic demand.[12]

Inculturation as incarnation

The statement quoted above reflects the belief that God transcends culture but works through culture for, in both the Old Testament and the New Testament,

> God's message of salvation is not communicated to human beings in a vague general way but in concrete human situations and through the resources of the culture of the people to whom it is given. Inculturation is rooted in this consciousness that God relates to people within the context of their life situation and culture.[13]

The pre-eminent example of this is the incarnation of the one and only Son of God (John 1:14; Heb 2:14–18). As a Jewish boy, raised in Galilee, Jesus grew up steeped in the traditions of his people. There can be no doubt that he was part of a cultural community. He proclaimed the Good News to the Jewish people from within the perspective of the Jewish culture, and he challenged that culture to respond by using its resources to express the message of salvation.[14] This is clear both from the gospel narratives and from Paul's statement that Jesus was "born of

12. Uzukwu, *Liturgy*, 27–28.
13. Ukpong, "Inculturation and Evangelization", 9.
14. Justin S. Ukpong, "Christology and Inculturation: A New Testament Perspective", in *Paths of African Theology*, ed. Rosino Gibellini (Maryknoll, NY: Orbis, 1994), 44–58.

a woman, born under the law" (Gal 4:4). In other words, he was born as a human being and specifically as a Jew.

Inculturation and the Last Supper

We see evidence of Jesus's roots in a cultural community in the final meal Jesus shared with his disciples before he died.[15] This Last Supper, which we as a Christian community re-enact in the Lord's Supper, was probably a Passover meal, which Jesus and his disciples would have celebrated in the form that had become part of Jewish culture in New Testament times.[16]

When God delivered Jesus's Jewish ancestors from Egypt, he commanded Moses; "This day shall be a day of remembrance for you. You shall celebrate it as a festival to the LORD; throughout your generations you shall observe it as a perpetual ordinance" (Exod 12:14). Moses and Aaron were given detailed instructions about how to observe the Passover (Exod 12:1–20, 24–27; Deut 16:1–4). These instructions specified that it should be celebrated on the fifteenth day of the month of Nisan and that it should include a meal. So,

> during the afternoon of what would be the same day by our reckoning but was the end of the fourteenth day by the Jewish reckoning, the lambs which were intended for the consumption at the Passover meal were brought to the temple and there they were personally slain by the persons offering them instead of, as was usual, by the priests.[17] The priests took the blood from

15. Jerome Kodell, *The Eucharist in the New Testament* (Collegeville, MN: Liturgical Press, 1988), 22. See also A. J. B. Higgins, *The Lord's Supper in the New Testament* (London: SCM, 1952), 9; Robert J. Daly, *Christian Sacrifice: The Judaeo-Christian Background before Origen* (Washington, DC: Catholic University of America Press, 1978), 499.

16. The outline given below is abridged from Marshall, *Last Supper*, 21–23. Two important Jewish feasts overlapped and were consequently celebrated together. The Feast of Unleavened Bread (lasting seven days) overlapped the Passover feast. Both feasts were celebrated in the Jewish month of Nisan (equivalent to March or April in our calendar). Other Passover outlines of comparable significance detailing the key elements of the Passover as celebrated by Jews of Jesus's time can be found in J. Jeremias, *The Eucharistic Words of Jesus*, 2nd ed., trans Arnold Ehrhardt (Oxford: Blackwell, 1955), 57–60; Heron, *Table and Tradition*, 21; William Barclay, *The Lord's Supper* (London: SCM, 1967), 20–24.

17. Barclay disagrees, stating that the Passover lamb was slain by the priest, as was the case in other

> the slaughtered animals and poured it out at the foot of the altar of burnt offering. Then the people gathered together in family groups or in *ad hoc* gatherings of friends, at least ten in number, to celebrate the meal after sunset.[18]

This pattern was laid down in the Torah. Other details of the celebration were not. For example, at the beginning of the Passover meal, the head of the household said a prayer of thanksgiving before serving the first of the four cups of wine served at various stages of the Passover meal. These cups represented the four promises of Exodus 6:6–7: "I will free you from the burdens of the Egyptians and deliver you from slavery to them. I will redeem you with an outstretched arm and with mighty acts of judgment. I will take you as my people and I will be your God."[19]

The meal began with greens, bitter herbs and *haroseth* sauce (a mixture of fruits and sauces in vinegar) to remind the people of their days of hardship in Egypt. Then, in accordance with the Torah, there would be a recounting of the events of the redemption symbolized in the Passover meal. A son would begin the story by asking the father why the night was different from others and by asking about the significance of the constituents of the meal: why seasoned food was served twice and not once as was usually the case, why unleavened bread was served instead of leavened bread, and why only roast meat instead of the usual combination of roasted, stewed and cooked meat? The father's response, drawn from Deuteronomy 26:5–11, would begin "a wandering Aramean was my ancestor . . .".

The second course of the meal would be served with the second cup of wine, with grace being said over the unleavened bread, which was now served for the first time in the course of the meal. Sometimes, if the main course had not yet been served, it was served at this point. The main course consisted of the roasted Passover lamb, served with bitter herbs and fruit puree. A third cup of wine (also called the cup of blessing) was served, again accompanied by a grace. A dessert course, which would have been served by this time in a normal meal, was omitted in the Passover meal. A fourth and final cup of wine was then served to

---

blood sacrifices (*The Lord's Supper*, 18).

18. I. H. Marshall, *Last Supper and Lord's Supper*, 21.

19. Barclay, *The Lord's Supper*, 21–22.

the guests though it is doubtful whether this custom goes back to the time of Jesus.[20] When all the eating and festivities were done, the guests were expected to spend the night in prayer.

Marshall states that the Passover feast was "one of remembrance and praise to God for his redemption of the people of Israel from Egypt. It also became an occasion for looking forward to the future redemption which God would bring through the Messiah".[21] For Heron, the Passover feast was "a feast of liberation, and marked as such by the fact that a quite exceptional quantity of wine – four cups in all – was drunk. It was also a meal at which Jews then would commonly recline on couches rather than sit on chairs, thus symbolizing their status as free people, freed by God himself".[22]

Those who are inclined to argue about details of the way the Lord's Supper is to be celebrated on the basis of the New Testament text should note that Jesus did not object to celebrating the Passover in a form that was not identical with that laid down in Exodus 12. The Passover feast had become deeply inculturated, but the spiritual meaning of the celebration was retained in the additions that had been made over the centuries since the exodus.

Although the New Testament does not give us a full account of the Last Supper, Matthew, Mark and Luke do give us enough details to persuade most scholars that what they ate was some kind of Passover meal.[23] N. T. Wright says:

> It seems to me virtually certain that the meal in question was some kind of Passover meal [for it] was eaten at night, and in Jerusalem; Jesus and his followers normally returned to Bethany for the night, but Passover meals had to be eaten within the city limits and after dark . . . The meal ended with a hymn, presumably the Hallel psalms sung at the end of the Passover

20. Luke's Gospel reflects a different arrangement – one cup preceded the breaking of the bread and another cup was shared after the sharing of the bread (Luke 22:17–20).

21. Marshall, *Last Supper*, 23.

22. Heron, *Table and Tradition*, 21. It is, however, difficult to ascertain whether peasants had chairs. The wealthy may have had them since the rich and powerful often sat on a *thronos* or chair.

23. Marshall, *Last Supper*, 23; Higgins, *The Lord's Supper*, 13, 45, 51. However, Eduard Schweizer, while acknowledging an inherent relationship between the Last Supper and the Passover tradition, does not take it to mean that the two are necessarily or obviously linked (*The Lord's Supper According to the New Testament* [Philadelphia: Fortress, 1967], 32).

> meal . . . The best explanation for Jesus' crucial words is that the head of the household would normally explain certain parts of the Passover meal in relation to the exodus narrative. . . . Passover would normally be celebrated by families.[24]

Jesus's taking this Jewish festival that commemorates deliverance from slavery through the death of a sacrificial lamb (and of the firstborn in Egypt) and transforming it into a commemoration of his own death is a vivid example of divine inculturation, "not in a way that falsifies the message, but in the way in which the message is formulated and interpreted anew".[25]

Inculturation and the Lord's Supper

Given that Jesus came as a Jew, and that Christians are called to be like him, does everyone who becomes a Christian need to become Jewish like him? This was a question the New Testament church wrestled with. The answer was revealed to Peter in his vision on a rooftop in Joppa (Acts 10:9–15), where God told him that the cultural issues that were so important to Jews (what foods could or could not be eaten, and not associating with Gentiles or visiting their homes) were no longer relevant. The issue came to a head around the time of the Council of Jerusalem in Acts 15, when it was explicitly decided by the early church leaders that Gentile converts to Christ did not have to become Jewish in their culture. They recognized that Jesus's resurrection implied that he had "'passed over' to a completely new form of life, the life of God, of the Spirit, which transforms his human reality into the 'new creation'. The risen Lord is thus the meeting-place of all peoples".[26]

The same reasoning underpins Paul's argument against the necessity of circumcision for Gentile believers in Christ (Gal 2). Paul also dismisses the Jewish emphasis on matters of food and drink; observance of festivals, new moons and Sabbaths; the worship of angels; visions and the like (Col

---

24. N. T. Wright, *Jesus and the Victory of God* (Minneapolis: Fortress, 1996), 554–559. Daly, *Origins*, 38, states, "The first Christians looked upon the Christ-event as a Passover event."
25. Shorter, *Toward a Theology of Inculturation*, 13–14.
26. Brian Hearne, "Christology and Inculturation", *African Ecclesiastical Review* (*AFER*) 22 (1980): 339.

2:16–19). These tenets of Jewish spirituality were not to be transported to other cultures where the risen Lord had incarnated.

The fact that Christ is now in us, as Paul would say (see, for example, Col 2:17), means that through us he is incarnate in our own cultures. We can proclaim the risen Lord as one who is able to incarnate in all human cultures in every time and every place. That is why he is able to communicate effectively with people of all nations and effect the eternal salvation for which he came in the first place. The risen Lord then challenges other cultures just as he challenged the Jewish culture at the time of his historical incarnation.

Can you now see why incarnation is a suitable theological model for understanding inculturation?

> It means that as Christ himself chose to become man in order to save humanity, Christianity has no alternative but to do the same in every culture and time in order to continue the salvation. . . . Inculturation means the honest and serious attempt to make Christ and his message of salvation ever more understood by peoples of every culture, locality and time. It means the reformulation of Christian life and doctrine into the very thought patterns of each people. . . . The permanence of Christianity will stand and fall on the question of whether it has become truly African: whether Africans have made Christian ideas part of their own thinking, whether Africans feel that the Christian vision of life fulfils their own needs, whether the Christian world view has become part of truly African aspirations. . . . Inculturation, therefore, is that movement which aims at making Christianity permanent in Africa by making it a people's religion and a way of life which no enemy or hostility can ever succeed in supplanting or weakening.[27]

Some criticize incarnation as a theological model for understanding inculturation, saying that it diverts Christians from their faith in Christ and directs them into paths of paganism, superstition and the type of syncretistic Christianity that has long been condemned by the church.[28]

---

27. Waliggo et al., *Inculturation*, 11–13.
28. Waliggo et al., 13.

While this danger is real and one we need to be alert to, this does not mean that we should shun the path of inculturation. To do so would simply drive inculturation underground, where it would proceed without any theological direction or oversight.

Either we incarnate the gospel among the African peoples or we continue with the *status quo* where churchgoers have a split personality: one African and one Christian. During times of joy and peace, such Christians live as Christians, but in times of dire need (e.g. disease, suffering, death, barrenness) they revert to the rituals and ceremonies of their African world view – even though these have long been condemned by the church.[29] So they will do this secretly, because the majority of Christians on the African continent have been socialized to reject their own cultures and cultural practices because these were considered evil by those who brought the Western form of Christianity to Africa. For example, in 1902, Fr. Parlo of the Consolata Fathers described the culture of the Kikuyu people of Kenya as "essentially deplorable, barbarous and inhuman".[30]

Africans should not have to live in shame, hate and denial. There is nothing to be ashamed of really, except that we have allowed ourselves to be brainwashed. Our faith is in God who was already with us and at work in our cultures before the missionaries came to Africa. African Christians should not have to "be secretive about all forms of their indigenous religious heritage, some of which may not fundamentally be in contradiction to the Christian faith, when this is understood as the will of God as expressed in the life and teachings of Jesus Christ".[31]

How do we go about encouraging Christians in Africa not to be ashamed of their cultures and cultural practices but to bring them to Christ and allow him to work on them and transform them, as he transformed the Jewish culture in which he grew up? One way to do this is to incarnate the sacrificial death of Christ in the Christian sacrament of the Lord's Supper. It has been said that "in the gift of the Eucharist we are meant to find ourselves in the narrative of Jesus's death and resurrection

29. Waliggo et al., 22.

30. Nahashon W. Ndung'u, "Cultural Challenges and the Church in Africa", *African Ecclesiastical Review* (*AFER*) 50, no. 1–2 (March–June 2008): 75.

31. Magesa, "Christian Faith and African Culture", 3, 4.

and to see that his story continues in our lives".[32] But how can Jesus's story continue in our own lives unless he is incarnated in us?

It is high time for us to find practical ways in which the Lord's Supper can be inculturated in socio-cultural groups across Africa. In the next chapters, we will look at ways in which this could be done in order to help African peoples to understand and appreciate better the significance of the work of Christ as celebrated in the Christian sacrament of the Lord's Supper.

32. R. K. Seasoltz, "Human Victimization and Christ as Victim in the Eucharist", *Worship* 76, no. 2 (March 2002): 121.

5

THE LANGUAGE OF SACRIFICE

Traditional African life is very ritualistic, both in religious and non-religious contexts, and some elements of these rituals remain today. Moreover, sacrifice is at the centre of the religious life of the majority of the socio-cultural groups in Africa, so that the symbolism of blood in African sacrificial systems and in the blood relationship rituals of the African is well understood. Blood sacrifices are still being offered for fertility, fecundity, healing, wealth creation and sustainability. In the recent past, cases of blood sacrifices have been reported for ascending to and retaining political office or jobs.

But the Protestant missionaries who came to Africa introduced a faith devoid of ritual and played down the sacrificial elements of Christ's death and of the Lord's Supper. In so doing, they missed out on important means of discipling their converts. Why did they do this, and what can be done to remedy the situation?

Avoidance of Sacrificial Language

At the time of the Reformation in the sixteenth century, the idea that the Lord's Supper was closely linked to sacrifice became linked to the great controversy about the exact meaning of the word "is" when Christ said, "This is my body". The Roman Catholic Church held firmly to the doctrine of transubstantiation, which holds that when the priest says the prayer of consecration, the substance of the bread and wine is transformed into the substance of the body and blood of Christ. The elements may continue to look like bread and wine, but their appearance does not reflect their true substance. A closely related idea is that the celebration of the Eucharist is itself a propitiatory sacrifice – the same sacrifice Christ offered on the cross for the sins of both the living and the dead. As the catechism explains: "As often as the sacrifice of the cross by which 'Christ our Pasch has been sacrificed' is celebrated on the altar, the work of redemption is carried out" (C1364).[1]

In such thinking, the sacrifice of Christ and the sacrifice of the Eucharist are seen as not two but one single sacrifice: "The victim is one and the same: . . . only the manner of offering is different" (C1367). Moreover, in Roman Catholic teaching, it is not only Christ who offers himself as a sacrifice:

> The Eucharist is also the sacrifice of the church. The church, which is the Body of Christ, participates in the offering of her Head. . . . The whole church is united with the offering and intercession of Christ. . . . To the offering of Christ are united not only the members still here on earth, but also those already in the glory of heaven. (C1367 – C1370)

Over time, the Eucharist itself came to be seen as having saving power, bestowed through the priest who celebrated it. Some priests exploited the power this conferred on them.[2]

The sixteenth-century Reformers objected to this teaching because they were convinced that people were saved by faith alone, grace alone and Scripture alone. There was no need for a human priest to act as an intermediary between God and sinners – all the more so given the scriptural teaching about the priesthood of all believers (1 Pet 2:9). While the Reformers disagreed among themselves on the details of eucharistic theology (see the appendix), it seems fair to say that they all agreed on the non-sacrificial character of the Eucharist.

This understanding led Protestants to downplay any sacrificial elements in the Lord's Supper. Thus when the CMS and other groups brought the gospel of Christ to Africa, they determinedly avoided any association of

1. The text I am working with is *The Catechism of the Catholic Church* (Nairobi: Pauline Publications Africa, 1994). Mambo Press jointly publishes this Catechism in Gweru, Zimbabwe. The section dealing with sacramental sacrifice is on pages 343–345.

2. M. Joseph Powers, *Eucharistic Theology* (New York: Herder & Herder, 1967), 33–34. Luther was highly critical of those who earned their living by celebrating mass in the chantries often referring to them in a derogatory manner as "fat bellies".

the Lord's Supper with sacrifice. Yet their strong stand against a sacrificial understanding of the Lord's Supper was more of a reaction against medieval eucharistic theology than a position reached on the basis of close analysis of the biblical text. After all, Paul makes much use of the language of sacrifice when speaking of the death of Christ[3] and so does the author of the book of Hebrews (Heb 9:1 – 10:18).[4] Moreover Jesus's words at the Last Supper are laden with sacrificial imagery.

The Language of Sacrifice at the Last Supper

The Last Supper was the meal at which Jesus introduced the ritual use of bread and wine to his followers, and so laid the foundations for our celebration of the Lord's Supper. As was pointed out in the chapter on inculturation, the meal at which Jesus did this was probably the Passover meal. Although this was a meal of thanksgiving and remembrance, it also had a strong association with sacrifice, for the slaughter of the Passover lambs was a key element in the feast:

> [D]uring the afternoon . . . the lambs which were intended for the consumption at the Passover meal were brought to the temple and there they were personally slain by the persons offering them instead of, as was usual, by the priests. The priests took the blood from the slaughtered animals and poured it out at the foot of the altar of burnt offering. Then the people gathered together in family groups or in *ad hoc* gatherings of friends, at least ten in number, to celebrate the meal after sunset.[5]

While the death of these lambs is not presented as a sacrifice for sin, it was

3. See 1 Thess 5:9–10; Gal 1:4; 2:20; 3:13; 1 Cor 5:7; 15:13; 2 Cor 5:14–15, 21; Rom 3:24–26; 4:25; 5:6–8; 8:3, 32; Eph 1:7; 2:13; 5:2; 5:25.

4. See Hebrews 9:1 – 10:18. For details of the use and meanings of the various sacrificial terms in Hebrews, see Edison Muhindo Kalengyo, "The Sacrifice of Christ and Ganda Sacrifice: A Contextual Interpretation in Relation to the Eucharist", in R. J. Bauckham, D. R. Driver, T. A. Hart and N. MacDonald, eds., *The Epistle to the Hebrews and Christian Theology* (Grand Rapids, MI: Eerdmans, 2009), 302–318. See also Edison Muhindo Kalengyo, *Sacrifice in Hebrews and the Pauline Epistles* (Nairobi: Acton, 2015), 45–221.

5. I. H. Marshall, *Last Supper and Lord's Supper*, 21. Barclay, however, says that the Passover lamb, like other blood sacrifices, was slain by the priest (*The Lord's Supper*, 18).

still a sacrifice that was an essential element in the delivery of the Israelites from slavery and in the commemorative annual feast that celebrated that delivery (see Exod 12).

Jesus's words show that he was clearly aware of this sacrificial element. The gospels tell us that he began by offering a prayer of thanksgiving as a way of acknowledging God's goodness. This would have been standard practice in a Jewish Passover celebration. What was unique, however, was how Jesus interpreted what he was doing: "He took a loaf of bread, and when he had given thanks, he broke it and gave it to them, saying, 'This is my body, which is given for you. Do this in remembrance of me'" (Luke 22:19).

How are we to interpret his actions and his words? Theologians have long argued about whether the word "is" should be interpreted literally or figuratively.[6] Here, however, we will focus on the word "body" (*soma* in Greek). This word can be used to refer to a person (in the same way as the English word "somebody" refers to a person, and not just to their body). If that is the way Jesus is using it here, then he is saying that he is giving them himself, his whole person. Similar language was used in the Old Testament and other Jewish writings to refer to those who sacrifice themselves on behalf of others. For example, Isaiah speaks of the suffering servant of the Lord who suffers and dies in order to "make many righteous and . . . bear their iniquities (Isa 53:11). The book of Maccabees says that Eleazar who died in battle "gave his life to save his people" (1 Macc 6:28–47).

However, the word *soma* can also be used to refer to flesh as distinct from bones and blood. In Jewish sacrifices, these two elements were separated. We see this in passages like Leviticus 4:5–12, where different instructions are given with regard to the way the blood and flesh of sacrificial animals were to be disposed of. If this is the context Jesus has in mind, he is saying that he is sacrificially giving up his life and that the breaking of the bread refers to the violent nature of his death.[7] This

6. In other words, does the "is" mean "signifies" (symbolic interpretation), or does it mean "identical with" (literal interpretation). Kodell comments: "For us, the word 'symbolic' is often used in contradiction to 'real', and a symbol is an action or object that stands metaphorically for something else. To the Hebrew mind, symbols were realities in their own right, the prophetic word made visible. The symbolic action in some sense brought the event into existence" (*The Eucharist*, 63).

7. This is the view held by Joseph M. Powers, who argues that "body and blood are sacrificial

interpretation is supported by the clear parallelism of the bread and the cup sayings in Mark's Gospel:

> While they were eating, he took a loaf of bread, and after blessing it he broke it, gave it to them, and said, "Take; this is my body." Then he took a cup, and after giving thanks he gave it to them, and all of them drank from it. He said to them, "This is my blood of the covenant, which is poured out for many." (Mark 14:22–24)

In the Bible, references to "blood" are almost always set in the context of death (especially violent death) and sacrifice.[8] Clearly what Jesus is speaking of at the Last Supper encompasses both ideas, for he will shortly die a violent death on the cross, and the idea of blood being "poured out" for another is closely associated with the sacrifices in which an animal was slaughtered on behalf of a worshipper or worshippers.

Mark's gospel also links the shedding of Christ's blood with the concept of covenant, for Jesus refers to the wine as "my blood of the covenant" (Mark 14:24). Covenants too were ratified by the shedding of sacrificial blood, as can be seen when God enters into a covenant with Abraham (Gen 15:9, 18). However, given that the Last Supper was a Passover meal, it seems far more likely that the covenant Christ alludes to was the covenant between God and his people that was made at Sinai. That covenant too was inaugurated with the blood of a sacrifice, which Moses dashed on the people, saying, "See the blood of the covenant that the Lord has made with you in accordance with all these words" (Exod 24:8). The significance of Christ's linking his own blood with the Sinai covenant is clear:

> The sacrifice which inaugurated the covenant in the wilderness was intended to atone for the sins of the people so that they might then belong to God in a covenant relationship. The blood thrown on the altar by Moses had atoning effects. The

---

realities" (*Eucharistic Theology*, 61). Bruce Chilton is more explicit: "Wine was his blood of sacrifice and bread was his flesh of sacrifice (*Jesus' Prayer and Jesus' Eucharist: His Personal Practice of Spirituality* [Valley Forge, PA: Trinity Press International, 1997], 73). See also Jeremias, *Eucharistic Words*, 144. Note that Marshall (*Last Supper*, 86) warns against interpreting the breaking of bread as symbolizing solely the breaking of the body of Christ in death.

8. Marshall, *Last Supper*, 91.

> sacrifice was in effect the means authorized by God for cleansing the people from their sins. By analogy therefore, Jesus here interprets his own death as a substitutionary sacrifice for the sins of the people that they may become partakers in the new covenant.[9]

Luke too stresses that Christ linked his death with a covenant – "the new covenant in my blood" (Luke 22:20). His hearers would have been reminded of Jeremiah's prophecy that God was going to make a new covenant with his people – a covenant that would supersede and render obsolete his previous covenants with them (Jer 31:31–34). Jesus is here saying that his sacrificial death inaugurates that covenant.

Given all that said above, how can we deny that there were sacrificial overtones at the institution of the Lord's Supper? Why then should we deny these in our celebrations of that supper today?

Implications and Applications of Sacrificial Language at the Last Supper

After looking at the bread and cup sayings in the New Testament narratives, we can see that the sacrifice associated with the Last Supper can be described as a gift, as substitutionary, representational, vicarious, atoning, and covenantal, and as communion. In all these various understandings of the nature of the sacrifice of the Last Supper, Christ is the only mediator and agent of sacrifice.

What do these words mean for how we celebrate the Lord's Supper? Let us look at four of them, and see how the concepts they represent are incorporated in the eucharistic liturgies of various African churches.

The bread and wine are a gift

After giving thanks for the bread and the wine, Jesus gives them to his disciples, who take and eat the bread and drink the wine. He offers a gift, and his disciples accept what he has offered. This may not seem an important point, but we should note that by accepting the gift that Jesus gives, "the disciples accepted the symbolical significance of the gift and

9. Marshall, 92.

thus gave their assent to that offer".[10] So when we celebrate the Lord's Supper, we should make it clear that this ritual involves a sacrificial gift symbolizing Jesus's offer of salvation, and that we accept this gift.

One way in which this point can be brought out is by asking people to come forward to receive the bread and wine. This is standard practice in Anglican and Roman Catholic Churches, but in some Protestant churches the congregation remain seated as the bread and the wine are passed around the church. While that approach is not wrong, it may sometimes be a good idea to ask people to come forward to receive the elements as a gift.

We could also consider encouraging the congregation to receive the elements using whatever gesture is appropriate when receiving a gift. For example, some Shona people gently clap their hands together before accepting the gift with both hands. We should welcome and encourage such gestures when receiving the bread and the wine at the Lord's Supper.

The bread and wine represent an atoning sacrifice

Luke stresses that the bread Jesus offers "is given for you" and that the cup he offers is "poured out for you" (Luke 22:19–20). No sacrificial animal dies for its own sake; it is always slaughtered on behalf of some individual or community. In the same way, Jesus does not die for his own sake, in order to earn some personal merit; he dies for the sake of others. To put this in theological language, his sacrifice is representative or vicarious.[11]

Matthew makes the same point even more strongly: "this is the blood of the covenant, which is poured out for many for the forgiveness of sins" (Matt 26:28). His words make it clear that the sacrifice being spoken of at the Last Supper is an atoning sacrifice. This statement fits very well with the prophecy regarding the role of the suffering servant who "bore the sin of many" (Isa 53:12). Jesus's vicarious death was not just for the small group of disciples who were present at the Last Supper but was for all who follow him. He had not only come to restore the Jews but had been given by God "as a light to the nations that my salvation may reach to the end of the earth" (Isa 49:6).

---

10. Marshall, 85.
11. See Jeremias, *Eucharistic Words*, 148–152, for a detailed explanation.

Given that the Roman Catholic Church refers to what Protestants call the Lord's Supper as the "eucharistic sacrifice", it is the Roman Catholic Church that has been most successful in reminding African worshippers that this ritual relates to Christ's sacrificial death on the cross. We can see this clearly if we compare the eucharistic liturgies of the Roman Catholic Church and the Anglican Church in Uganda.

The liturgy of the Roman Catholic Church in Uganda is set out in the *Ekitabo Ky'omukristu* and the *Enneegayirira ezimu Ez'abakristu.*[12] It uses the word *ekitambiro* when speaking of Christ's sacrifice.[13] This is the traditional Luganda word for a ritual sacrifice that involves the shedding of blood. Such sacrifices traditionally established communication, communion and friendship between the visible and the invisible world and averted all forms of evil.[14]

By contrast, the Anglican liturgy set out in the Luganda Prayer and Hymn Book (LPHB) refers to Christ's sacrificial death using the word *ssaddaaka.*[15] This word traditionally refers to offerings or sacrifices that do not involve the shedding of blood, and its use weakens people's understanding of Christ's giving his body and blood for many. (*Ssaddaaka* is, however, the correct translation for non-ritual sacrifices like the psalmist's "sacrifice of thanksgiving" [Ps 50:14] and Paul's exhortation to offer our bodies as "a living sacrifice" [Rom 12:1]).[16]

Similarly, the two liturgies divide over the use of the word *kabona*, which used to refer to the type of "priest" who presided over ritual sacrifices in Ganda traditional religion. While the Roman Catholic liturgy

---

12. *Ekitabo Ky'omukristu* (Kisubi: Marianum Press Kisubi, 1975) is a large volume (847 pages) that sets out all the various services and readings for the entire church year. The Eucharist is dealt with on pages 644–692. The *Enneegayirira ezimu Ez'abakristu,* 9th ed. (Kisubi: Marianum Press Kisubi, 1990) is a short (94 pages) booklet that contains the central elements of the Mass and is the version that most Christians would use. The Eucharist is dealt with on pages 17–48.

13. See *Enneegayirira*, 28, 31; *Ekitabo Ky'omukristu*, 644, 657, 658, 673, 688.

14. Ganda cosmology recognizes a visible world (human beings, animals, trees and everything that can be touched, felt or seen) and an invisible spirit world. The spirit world was seen as having unlimited access to and control of the visible world, but the visible world does not ordinarily have the privilege of influencing (let alone having access to) anything in the spirit world. Traditional sacrifices were offered to various deities in an attempt to bridge this gap and change the status quo. No sacrifices were offered to or expected by the Supreme Being.

15. The LPHB (Kampala: Uganda Bookshop, 1977) preserves the pattern and structure of the 1662 Anglican Book of Common Prayer (BCP). Any revisions focus on the clarification of Luganda terms or using simpler synonyms while retaining the eucharistic theology of the 1662 BCP.

16. The word is used correctly in LPHB, 79, 81.

uses this term, the Anglican liturgy uses the word *omukadde*, which simply means "old person" or "elder". There are good reasons for this choice, not least that it is the form often used in the New Testament. But one of the side-effects of the attempt to reduce any danger of syncretism is that there is also a reduced understanding that the Lord's Supper represents a sacrifice. This makes it more difficult to explain the meaning of the Eucharist to the faithful and show its relationship to the Christian community (the body of Christ) and the risen Lord. Increasingly people (especially the young) are beginning to question the relevance of the Eucharist in Christian life and worship.

The bread and wine represent a covenant sacrifice

All four accounts of the institution of the Lord's Supper see it as a covenant sacrifice. Matthew and Mark refer to the cup as the "blood of the covenant" (Matt 26:28; Mark 14:24), while in Luke and Paul it is "the new covenant in my blood" (Luke 22:20; 1 Cor 11:25). Covenant blood was always the blood of a sacrifice. Thus the sacrifice of the Last Supper is to be understood as a new covenant sacrifice in that it inaugurates the new covenant in the blood of Christ that replaces the old covenant of Sinai. It is also to be seen as the fulfilment of Jeremiah's prophecy (Jer 31:31–34).

What this means is that Christ's sacrificial death brings all who believe in him into God's covenant people. As those who have become members of his family of promise, we celebrate what was done and so participate in the Lord's Supper.

The Eucharist involves communion and fellowship

In the words of institution at the Last Supper, Jesus was saying, "This is myself: by sharing this meal with you I am bringing you into an intimate relationship with myself." This leads to the following conclusion: "Sharing the bread and wine unites us to Jesus as he is now, the risen Lord in glory."[17] This is the element of communion in the Last Supper, something that Paul emphasizes in his rhetorical question in 1 Corinthians:

> The cup of blessing that we bless, is it not a sharing in the blood of Christ? The bread that we break, is it not a sharing in the

17. Kodell, *The Eucharist*, 63.

> body of Christ? Because there is one bread, we who are many are one body, for we all partake of one bread. (1 Cor 10:16–17)

When we share in the Lord's Supper, we become intimately united to Jesus Christ and his life bonds us into one body. We will look at the implications of this in more detail in chapter 9.

Conclusion

The avoidance of explicit sacrificial language in the Anglican liturgy has made it more difficult to explain the meaning of the Lord's Supper to the faithful and show its relationship to the Christian community and to the risen Lord. The result has been that believers (especially younger believers) no longer grasp the importance of the Eucharist in Christian life and worship. While addressing language issues will not solve this problem on its own, it would be a move in the right direction. There are, however, also other language issues that we need to address in relation to the way we celebrate the Lord's Supper.

6

WESTERN LANGUAGES AND AFRICAN LITURGIES

Language is not a neutral artefact. The language we speak is a vital part of our identity. It is both a means of communication and the tool we use to instruct the young in the norms and values of our culture. In my home country (Uganda), primary schools are now required to teach in the children's mother tongue because research has shown that it is easier for older children to understand new and complex concepts if they have received a thorough grounding in their own culture and language. If this is true in the educational sphere, it is also true in the church.

Western Languages

What language to use when celebrating the Lord's Supper has been a contentious issue in the West. For centuries, the Roman Catholic Church insisted that the only acceptable language was Latin. It was only in the twentieth century that it came to accept that the Mass could be celebrated in the vernacular, and there are still pockets of resistance to this change. Similarly, there have been complaints each time there has been a change in the Anglican order of service.

This concern for language is not rooted simply in conservatism and resistance to change, although these may play a part. A more important concern is that the exact words used in a liturgy are important. They were chosen over the years with careful attention to the theological content of each word.

When missionaries established churches in Africa, they used Western liturgies. Even today, the liturgies used across Africa are often little more than translations of foreign texts. For example, the preface to the *Luganda Prayer and Hymn Book* indicates that it has its roots in the 1662 Anglican *Book of Common Prayer*. In 1898 this book was translated into Luganda by George Pilkington, with the help of Henry Wright Luttamaguzi Kitaakule. Newer editions were published in 1928 and 1932 and 1977, but all are based on the British text. In the Anglican and Catholic churches, any liturgical changes have to be approved by churches in the West.

Two other factors besides a concern for doctrinal correctness have also played into the African church's reliance on Western liturgies. One was practical – the missionaries who came to Africa lacked an adequate knowledge of the African languages, and so they used the languages they knew and conducted worship in English, French or Latin.

The other, more disturbing factor was the hostility of both Protestant and Roman Catholic missionaries to African traditional cultures, including African languages and the language used in worship. Two Luganda prayer books used in the Roman Catholic Church still refer to God using the Latin word "Pater" rather than the Luganda word for "Father".[1] In doing this, they misrepresent the word that Christ himself used in prayer. We know from Mark 14:36 that the word he used was *Abba*, the everyday word for "father". He used the language of his people, not an archaic term from another language. I find it hard to imagine Jesus Christ walking the villages of Buganda speaking Latin to the Ganda!

The problem with relying on a translated form of liturgy is that there is seldom a one-to-one correlation between the meanings of words in two different languages. There are some words in our mother tongues that express a certain idea far more clearly than any alien English word. And every language has certain words that are considered particularly significant, even sacred. Such words are often associated with the divine and ritual sacrifice. It is folly to ignore these connections. By doing so in our translations of the liturgy, we have allowed the Lord's Supper to

---

1. *Ekitabo Ky'omukristu* and *Enneegayirira ezimu Ez'abakristu*, 9th ed. (Kisubi: Marianum Press Kisubi, 1990).

remain foreign in character and foreign to the lived realities of the socio-cultural groups in Africa.

Churches across Africa are increasingly recognizing that we cannot simply translate the words of an English or Latin ritual into an African language and hope to communicate with the people.

African Liturgies

There is an urgent need for liturgies that truly reflect the distinctive cultural experiences of African worshippers. African liturgies need to be written in Africa by Africans for the African peoples. Only then will each socio-cultural group be able to express its lived realities without inhibition.

There are already examples of African liturgies which show that genuine liturgical inculturation is achievable. Take, for example, the Roman Catholic liturgy widely known as the Zairean Rite, which has an intimate connection with the culture of the Democratic Republic of Congo.[2] When this liturgy is celebrated, the priest dons robes and regalia more similar to those worn by a Congolese ruler than to those worn in Rome. All the servers are adults, and all carry spears like those carried by a chief's traditional guard. The entry of the priest and the servers is preceded by the entry of a man or woman who serves as an announcer or herald. Their role is modelled on that of a traditional herald who proclaims the arrival of an important person and directs people's responses. The lay announcer speaks at several places in the rite, acting as liaison between the priest and the congregation and encouraging the latter to participate in the worship.

When the priest and the servers enter the church, they do not do so in a solemn procession. Rather, they enter dancing and circle the altar, which is venerated on all four sides by the priest with his arms outstretched. The congregation too dance in place, just as they dance when coming to the altar to present their gifts. Their joy in worship is expressed in ways that have been familiar to Africans for generations.

2. The Zairean Rite was approved by the Holy See in April 1988, after having been in development since 1969. For details of the rite, see Nathan Peter Chase, "A History and Analysis of the Missel Romain les Dioceses du Zaire", *Obsculta* 6, no. 1 (2013): 28–36. Available online at http://digitalcommons.csbsju.edu/obsculta/vol6/iss1/14.

During the liturgy the invocation of the saints in the Roman rite is modified to include the invocation of the ancestors (more on this later in the book). Moreover, the proclamation and explication of the word of God are moved to precede the words of penitence and the sign of peace. This change in the order of the ritual is meant to remind the community that we come before God with rejoicing, but are then challenged by God's word, which moves us to penitence and brings about conversion.

It is abundantly clear that the liturgical expressions in the Zairean Rite truly express the fundamental truths of faith in the distinctive cultural experience of the Congolese people. This is as it should be for every socio-cultural group.

My own particular interest is in developing a liturgy for Uganda, one that takes into consideration the Ganda religious experience (and particularly their understanding of sacrifice). I have no doubt that this could be done, for Luganda is a rich language that can unambiguously convey theological meaning. For example, among the Ganda, the place of sacrifice (*itambiro*) was understood as a place of protection, cure and healing, which was understood not in terms of curing a specific disease but more in the Hebrew sense of general well-being in all aspects of life. The offering of a sacrifice (*ekitambiro*) was understood to bestow all these benefits. Should we not then imitate the Roman Catholics, who call the eucharistic celebration *Ekitambiro eky'Okwebaza* – literally "the sacrifice of thanksgiving". The presence of the word *ekitambiro* reminds them that it is Christ's sacrificial death that brings spiritual protection, cure and healing and fullness of life. Is this not a richness of theological depth that is missed when our liturgy does not use that word?

In the Ganda Roman Catholic eucharistic liturgy, the sacrifice of Christ is also referred to using the Ganda word *ekyonziira*, which refers to a traditional scapegoat sacrifice. The Ganda used to take sacrificial victims (both human and animal) to another region and sacrifice them there to avert wars and plagues and to purify the army after a military campaign. While these traditional Ganda sacrifices were often cruel in the way they were carried out, they were also clearly substitutionary or vicarious – the person or animal died so that the king and the nation would survive. In some respects, the fate of the sacrificial victim was similar to that of the Old Testament scapegoat, which was driven out into the wilderness on the Day of Atonement, symbolically carrying away the sins of the nation (Lev 16:7–10).

Could there be a clearer way to explain the sacrificial work of Christ, who offered himself as the sacrificial victim, taking upon himself the sin of his people, so that they could live free from evil? Should this word not have a place in our liturgies when we celebrate what Christ has done for us? Would the Ganda people not understand his work better if it were used?

By using the appropriate words we can teach all who participate in the Lord's Supper that Christ's death was a sacrifice that brings healing, protection, cure, and atonement for sin. We are missing out on a key teaching tool when we completely avoid traditional sacrificial language in our African liturgies.

Conclusion

Sacrificial language on its own is not enough. It may convey one thing in one culture and something else in another, and may even be misleading. When we use it, we need to be aware of the implicit religious ideas it conveys. We need to recognize that through it we can communicate a specific message about the inculturated Christ to the people of a particular culture. This message must not be cloaked in a foreign language that obscures the truth. Instead, we should use the language that is familiar to the people in a particular locality, while at the same time taking care to make sure that the theology of Christ's sacrifice for us shines out clearly.

7

THE FOOD OF THE PEOPLE

So far, we have been focusing primarily on the words used in our liturgical celebrations of the Lord's Supper. But we must not forget that almost all rituals involve gestures and symbolic objects, and the Lord's Supper is no exception.

Gestures are in essence body language with coded meaning. They are actions that convey a specific meaning in the context of a particular culture. For example, the Baganda kneel when greeting an elder or a leader to convey the message that they respect their age or their position. In some cultures, children may be told to keep their eyes down when being reprimanded to signal that they are paying attention to the authority figure. But in other cultures, an adult who is reprimanding a child will say. "Look at me when I talk to you!", for in that culture, eye contact signals respect. So we need to be aware of the gestures we use in our celebration of the Lord's Supper and of what those gestures mean in our own cultures. We touched on this earlier when I spoke about the gestures believers in some cultures might use as a reminder that the bread and the wine are Christ's gift to us.

Sometimes a gesture involves the use of a *symbolic object*. For example, in Egypt turning the sole of your shoe towards someone is an insult, a gesture of contempt, as we saw on our TV news during the unrest in Cairo in 2011. In this context, the sole of your shoe is not simply something you walk on; it is a symbolic object. Similarly, the bread and wine in the Lord's Supper are symbolic objects.

A *ritual* involves a set of gestures carried out by appropriate participants, often involving specific symbolic objects, to communicate a message that is understood both by the participants and by those observing the ritual. For example, in the ritual in which cultural leaders present someone with a spear or a stool, that spear or stool is a symbol that indicates the recipient's authority. But no such message would be conveyed if those doing the presentation were children playing a game – they are not appropriate participants in such a ritual.

Similarly, our celebrations of the Lord's Supper involve a chain of gestures, appropriate participants and the use of symbolic objects to communicate an important message. It is tragic that many do not hear this message because of the eucharistic famine in Africa. And even some of those who do take part in the Lord's Supper may not receive the full message because it is presented using gestures and symbols that do not communicate clearly in an African context.

Presenting the Bread and Wine

Jesus celebrated the Last Supper using bread and wine that others had prepared for the meal (Luke 22:7–13). It is thus appropriate that in the Roman Catholic Luganda liturgy the faithful carry the as yet unconsecrated bread and wine to the altar, together with other offertory gifts. At the altar, they are received by the presiding priest or bishop who then says:

> *Baganda bange mwegayirire, Katonda Patri omuyinza wa buli kantu, asiime ekitambiro nze nammwe kye tumuweereza.*[1]
>
> [Brethren, pray God the Father Almighty to accept the sacrifice you and I give to him.]

The people then respond:

> *Omukama ekitambiro ekyo akisiime, akiggye mu mikonogyo, akitwale, kiviiremu erinya lye ettendo n'ekitibwa naffe kitugase, wamu n'Eklezia yenna omutukuvu.*[2]

1. *Enneegayirira*, 31. Also see *Ekitabo Ky'omukristu*, 658.
2. *Enneegayirira*, 31. Also see *Ekitabo Ky'omukristu*, 658.

> [Let the Lord accept that sacrifice, receive it from your hands, take it, to the honour and glory of his name, and unite us together the whole holy Church.]

In taking the bread and wine to the altar, the faithful identify with the sacrifice they are offering to God: the bread and wine they offer are the fruit of their own labour. In offering them, the faithful demonstrate their desire to offer themselves to God. The sacrifice being offered is for the people and for the priest. It is evident from the people's response that their aspirations in offering the sacrifice are that God's name may be honoured and glorified and that through the sacrifice they may be united to the body of Christ – the entire Christian community called the church.

The presentation of the gifts is followed by the eucharistic prayer, which is dominated first by praise and thanksgiving to God for his saving work in Jesus Christ and then by the invocation of the Holy Spirit, who unites the self-offering of the faithful represented by their gifts of bread and wine to Christ's self-offering to God as sacrifice.

While the Anglican liturgy also allows for the bread and wine to be brought to the holy table by people representing the faithful, I have never witnessed this being done in all the services I have attended or participated in among the Ganda of the Anglican Church of Uganda. Nor does the liturgy mention any link between the bread and wine and the Christian community. Yet including this offering of the bread and wine in our liturgy would teach our people that they are not merely called to participate in Christ's sacrifice but also to continue it by offering the fruits of their labour to God.

But are bread and wine truly the fruits of African labour? Bread is generally not a staple food in Africa, and grapes are seldom grown here. So should we be celebrating the Lord's Supper using the Mediterranean staples of bread and wine, or should be using locally available food and drink?

Using Locally Available Food and Drink

Early in my pastoral ministry, long before I even heard about (let alone understood) the theological term "inculturation", I began to use pineapple and banana wine as elements in the celebration of the Lord's Supper. Both of these were readily available in the diocese of South Rwenzori in Uganda where I was stationed.

Some may dismiss that last sentence as unimportant. It is not. Both the availability and affordability of bread and wine, the traditional elements for the Lord's Supper, have remained high on the list of hindrances to the regular celebration of the Lord's Supper. Many African congregations are in rural areas, where it is not easy to buy wheat bread. After all, bread is not a regular item on the menu of many African rural homes, and there is no convenient delivery service. The situation is even worse when it comes to altar wine.

Then there is the issue of affordability. Imported altar wine and wheat bread are not cheap. Most rural churches cannot afford to buy them regularly. So why should we insist on celebrating the Lord's Supper using imported red wine and wheat bread. Why not consider the use of alternatives that are accessible and affordable in the places where the Christians live?

For some traditions and denominations this is considered a "no go" area. For example, look at what happened to Bishop Dupont of the Roman Catholic Diocese of Pala in the Chad Republic in the 1970s. There was a scarcity of imported wine, and so he celebrated the Eucharist with millet bread and millet beer. His colleagues complained to the authorities in Rome, and Bishop Dupont was relieved of his Episcopal duties.[3]

The closest the Anglican Communion has come to approving the use of locally available food and drink as alternative elements for the Eucharist was at the Lambeth Conference in 1908. At that time, the scarcity and unavailability of wine had led to a disruption in the regular celebration of the Eucharist in the Anglican Church of Uganda. Bishop Alfred Tucker, then Bishop of Uganda, argued at the Lambeth Conference for the use

3. Uzukwu Eugene, "Food and Drink in Africa", 370.

of palm wine in the celebration of Holy Communion.[4] He pointed out that wine (the pure juice of grapes) was expensive on the market and expensive to import. Additionally, Ugandans had been taught that wine and alcohol represented "peril to their physical, moral and spiritual lives".[5] Bishop Tucker called on the conference to address the "tremendous difficulty with which we are face to face".[6]

Others at the meeting expressed "concern . . . about the need to be like other catholic churches. There was fear that if anything else other than the juice of the grapes was authorized it would lead to a new cause of division and isolation".[7] Despite these concerns, the meeting unanimously acknowledged the seriousness of the pastoral problem that Bishop Tucker faced. They agreed as follows:

> The Bishop brought before us unmistakable, indisputable instance of absolute necessity, – that is to say, a case in which it was absolutely impossible to procure what is customary for use in the administration of the Holy Communion throughout the church.[8]

The following compromise resolution was adopted:

> The conference would urge emphatically that the greatest care should be taken to secure that the elements used in the Eucharist should be the purest wheaten bread that may conveniently be gotten and wine which shall be the pure juice of the grape. While urging this, the conference does not pronounce judgment upon such course as in case of absolute necessity may be in particular regions adopted by those Bishops on whom falls the responsibility of dealing with an imperative need.[9]

However, this resolution never saw the light of day. In his final decision, the Archbishop of Canterbury, the president of the Lambeth Conference, vetoed it. Thus the final declaration read as follows:

4. Lambeth Conference 1908 Minutes V 3–5 August – 13th Day. Proceedings of the Fifth Lambeth Conference (LC), Monday 3rd August 1908 – Lambeth Library Archives document LC 70:19–39.
5. LC 70:25–26.
6. LC 70:27.
7. LC 70:20.
8. LC 70:19.
9. LC 70:21.

> This conference declares that the only proper elements for use in the administration of the Holy Communion are bread and wine according to the institution of our Lord.[10]

This resolution seems to have ended official discussions on the use of locally available food and drink as alternative eucharistic elements in the Anglican Communion. It is, however, possible that there may have been further discussions of this issue in individual provinces of the Anglican Communion.

Unofficially, however, people have continued to talk about and even experiment with alternatives. I was not the only pastor in the diocese to use either banana wine or pineapple wine. In doing this, we were part of a long tradition, for it has been shown that historically eucharistic materials "can change and have not always remained the same in the Christian churches".[11] For example, prisoners of war have celebrated the Eucharist with water, biscuits and bread. In India there was a time when the Eucharist was celebrated with rice and tea. A Russian synod between 1589 and 1605 allowed cherry wine to be used for the Mass. And the First Provincial Synod of Milan in 1565 approved a shift from red wine to white wine.[12]

These historical precedents carry little weight with those who hold a dogmatic position on the use of wine and bread as symbols for the sacrificial death of Jesus Christ.[13] They argue, first, that unleavened bread must be used to remind the participants of the Passover meal (Exod 12) and God's deliverance of the Israelites from Egypt. Unleavened bread was an essential component of the Passover meal, and, as we have seen, it is highly probable that Jesus's Last Supper was a Passover meal. This being the case, we should eat the same type of bread as Jesus did. However, this argument falters because it seems that the early church did not focus on what type of bread was used. Those who gathered to celebrate the

10. LC 70:39.

11. Francois Kabasele Lumbala, *Celebrating Jesus in Africa: Liturgy and Inculturation* (Maryknoll, NY: Orbis, 1998), 52–53.

12. See Lumbala, *Celebrating Jesus in Africa*, 53 for details.

13. See also John Lukwata, *Integrated African Liturgy* (Eldoret: AMECEA Gaba, 2003), 83–84; Lumbala, *Celebrating Jesus in Africa*, 51–57.

Eucharist in the early church brought bread from their homes, and such bread would have been leavened.[14]

Those who insist on bread and wine also point to the fact that Jesus took bread and wine and instructed his disciples to do the same to remember him (Matt 26:26–28; Mark 14:22–24; Luke 22:14–20). They also point out that Jesus refers to himself as the bread of life (John 6:35, 48). Should we not then remember Jesus using the elements he instructed us to use? Is it not disobedience to use anything else?

They also argue that, apart from the isolated cases mentioned above, the Christian church in general has used bread made from wheat and red wine made from grapes to celebrate the Eucharist. And to those who argue that bread and wine from grapes are foreign to Africa, they respond that it is possible to grow grapes and wheat in many parts of Africa.

On the basis of these arguments, they insist that "the symbols of bread and wine in the Eucharist . . . used by Jesus at the Last Supper are irreplaceable".[15]

But the above arguments cease to be absolute in the face of the risen incarnate Lord Jesus. He identifies with all people in their varied cultures, and so one can no longer dogmatically prescribe bread and wine as being normative symbols of the eucharistic sacrifice.

The following quotation makes the point well:

> The Israelites, like any other people of the world, brought the fruit of their labour, all that formed their staple diet, into the cult [worship] of Yahweh. Wheat and barley were the principal agricultural products, and these figured prominently in their cult. . . . What constituted their food, the Israelites gave to God. . . . if this food had been millet, maize, yam, or cassava, it stands to reason that they would have offered the same. . . . Jesus could not change the Israelites' products of their land for imported cassava and palm-wine because cassava and palm-wine have no relation to Jewish life and religious experience.[16]

The risen Lord takes what he finds – what is available – and uses it to tell the central message of his death and resurrection. It ought to be

14. Lumbala, *Celebrating Jesus in Africa*, 51.
15. Okoye, "Eucharist in African Perspective", 164.
16. Uzukwu, "Food and Drink", 376.

appreciated that, "on the table of the disciples at Emmaus Jesus did not take out his own sandwich or picnic lunch. He took what the disciples had with them. He ate it in a new way that proclaimed his death and resurrection".[17]

We need to be relentless in our support of celebrating the Lord's Supper with African food and drink.

> Christ "for us" is our centre, our head; and he does not find it repugnant to eat what we eat, drink what we drink. In other words, he would find African food and drink more adequate to convey the memorial of his passion, death, and resurrection celebrated in the context of a meal on the continent, than imported material. First of all, these food items nourish Africans; and so they would form a natural parable for the spiritual nourishment and healing in the Eucharist. Secondly, these food items had been used in offerings and sacrifices in the traditional religion; therefore, they become instruments of symbolizing the recapitulation of all sacrifices of the past in Christ, and an establishment of the unique and acceptable sacrifice, the "pure offering" pleasing to God (Malachi 1:11). It follows then that millet, maize, rice, yam, cassava, banana, palm wine, millet beer, banana wine, honey beer are all potential elements in the eucharistic celebration.[18]

Think about the Ganda among whom I was ministering. They are an agricultural people and are largely dependent on agriculture. Fortunately, much of their land is arable. They grow plantain (bananas of various varieties), cassava, potatoes, beans (of various varieties), maize, millet, sorghum, pineapples, and fruit (mangoes, avocado and pawpaws/papayas).[19] But plantain is their staple food; so much so that the Ganda word for food (*emmere*), is identical with their word for plantain. To

17. Lumbala, *Celebrating Jesus in Africa*, 19–20.

18. Uzukwu, "Food and Drink", 381–382. Paul Gibson, who examined the various meals in which Jesus participated and their implications for Christian practice today, concluded that "in the activities of eating and drinking in which Jesus participated, the *act* of consuming food and drink together was primary while the commodity was secondary". Gibson too has argued for alternative eucharistic elements – see full article: Gibson Paul, "Forum: Eucharistic Food – May We Substitute?" *Worship* 76, no. 5 (September 2002): 445–455.

19. See Roscoe, *The Baganda*, 426–444.

invite someone for food is to imply that they will be served plantain. On a recent visit to Kampala, my wife and I were reminded of this when we invited our neighbours to share our lunch, only to have it returned to us. We realized that my wife had used the word *emmere*, but the food we had offered was potatoes. Even when other food is served, the Ganda will go away saying they never ate *emmere* (food) if plantain has not been served. It is central to the Ganda menu and a part of every Ganda festival and cultural celebration. If Jesus had attended a Ganda festival during his physical life on earth, he would have been served *emmere* (plantain). It is hard to imagine that Jesus would have turned it down and asked for Mediterranean food or unpacked his Mediterranean lunch!

In both the Roman Catholic and Anglican Ganda eucharistic liturgies, the word "bread" in the Lord's Prayer has been translated as *emmere*.[20] Why then should we insist that the Ganda eat bread when they come to the Lord's Supper?

Plantain as a food is often paired with plantain beer, which is the ordinary drink and is consumed at almost all cultural festivities.[21] If Jesus had been born among the Baganda, this is what he would have drunk. This was the beer used when offering libations to the Ganda deities. Why then do we insist on using grape wine rather than banana beer when celebrating the Lord's Supper? Why go to the enormous trouble and expense of trying to grow grapes in Uganda. Yet this is what the church has done. In 1908, at the height of discussions on the use of palm wine for eucharistic celebration in Uganda, it was reported to the Lambeth Conference

> We are not without hope that in the country itself we may be able to produce the wine. We have made experiments; . . . The Head of the Botanical Gardens at Entebbe has attempted to grow a certain kind of vine, and it is not beyond the bounds of possibility that it may be produced.[22]

Such efforts are uncalled for and have no biblical and theological basis.

---

20. Luganda Prayer and Hymn Book (1977), 75; *Enneegayirira ezimu Ez'abakristu* (1990), 36.
21. Different varieties of plantain are used for food and for brewing. For more details, see Roscoe, *The Baganda*, 431–442.
22. LC 70:27.

There is no need to burden African churches with the cost of purchasing bread and grape wine. For most African families, bread is a luxury item. While those in urban areas may be able to purchase bread and grape wine relatively easily, this is not the case for most rural parishes. Yet it is possible and cheap to process banana wine or fermented banana beer, which has a long storage life. There is even official precedent for this: "During the time of Amin in Uganda, when imported wine could not be got because of lack of foreign exchange, the House of Bishops of the Anglican Church of Uganda allowed the use of banana juice in some dioceses. And the Christians had no problem with it."[23]

The Ugandan government is currently running a project to process bananas, and according to the project coordinator it is possible to make banana bread and banana wafers.[24] I have been to homes where we have been served banana cakes. It has also been suggested that we should use "wafers made from maize flour (which is found all over Africa) and the local wine of the area as possible alternatives".[25] The point cannot be overemphasized, "The eucharist is not the sacrament of bread and wine but the sacrament of the death and resurrection of Christ. It is a memorial of his death and resurrection as a saving act, and not a memorial of Mediterranean agriculture".[26]

This problem is not unique to Uganda. In the Twi speaking area of Ghana, the references to bread in the liturgy for the Lord's Supper are translated as *paano*, using a word borrowed from the Portuguese who introduced wheat flour to the area in the sixteenth century. Yet in the translation of the Lord's Prayer, the word "bread" is translated as *aduane*, a word that refers to food derived from edible roots and grains such as yams and cassava. These are the staple foods in the area, the food that nourishes in Ghana. Not so "bread and wine". When praying the Lord's Prayer, no Twi speaker would ask God for *paano*, for no one considers it as food that nourishes the body. When they make offerings to God,

23. Elisha G. Mbonigaba, "The Indigenization of Liturgy", in *Anglican Liturgical Inculturation in Africa: The Kanamai Statement "African Culture and Anglican Liturgy"*, ed. David Gitari (Bramcote, Nottingham: Grove, 1994), 30. An earlier version of this article is "A Kingdom of Priests", in *Liturgical Formation of the People of God*, ed. Thomas J. Talley (Bramcote, Nottingham: Grove, 1988), 39–47.

24. Discussion with Dr Florence Muranga, Banana Processing Project Coordinator, Uganda.

25. Justin Ukpong, "Inculturation: A Major Challenge to the Church in Africa Today", 262.

26. Lumbala, *Celebrating Jesus in Africa*, 54.

the Twi bring bananas, oranges, corn, yams, money, live chickens and calabashes of palm wine. They do not bring wheat or wheat bread and grape wine.[27] The word *paano* is as foreign to them as the Mediterranean food it relates to and conveys no sense of the spiritual nourishment obtained from celebrating the Lord's Supper.

The following quotation sums up what I have been saying:

> Jesus said, "The human person was not made for the Sabbath, but the Sabbath for the person". Must one tie the worship of the community that follows him to the Mediterranean cultural customs and material forms for all eternity? Must one demand that the people of Africa and Asia say, "Blessed are you, God of the universe, you who give us this bread, fruit of the earth and the work of human hands," yet allow them to offer only the fruits of the Mediterranean basin? Certainly not. The God who is revealed to us in the gospels is not one who goes among the people as "Emmanuel", unpacking his "sandwich", and not eating the food of the people he is with. The God of Jesus Christ is not a God on a special diet who refuses to eat and drink what the people have.[28]

One way of inculturating the eucharistic sacrifice among Africans is through the use of locally available food and drink. What exactly will be used will vary across Africa. As we have seen, in Uganda people may use banana bread and banana beer or wine. This would be a true offering by the Ganda of the "fruit of the earth and work of human hands".

---

27. See further Jose Antunes da Silva, "Bread and Wine for the Eucharist: Are They Negotiable?" *African Ecclesiastical Review* (*AFER*) 34, no. 5 (1992): 259–262.
28. Lumbala, *Celebrating Jesus in Africa*, 56.

8

THE PLACE OF THE ANCESTORS

Among the regrettable blunders made by the early missionaries to the African peoples were their attempts to sever the bond between living African peoples and their ancestors. The African peoples are so inextricably linked with the ancestors that any attempt to deny this relationship is tantamount to denying them life itself. In the African worldview, individuals, families, clans cannot exist apart from the good will and continual support of the ancestors. It is no exaggeration to state that "ancestors in Africa are the 'principle' or 'source' of personal, family and community life".[1]

> Ancestors are believed to have continuous influence over the living members of their immediate kinship unit. Their influence can be positive or negative depending on the conduct of the living. They are believed to be the proprietors of the land, and are responsible for promoting the fertility of human beings and that of the earth and the growth of crops.[2]

Among the Baganda, for example, the role and influence of the ancestors was central to the life of the living. Sacrifices were regularly offered to keep them favourable to the living and to thank them for favours received. Pilgrimages were made to the shrines and to the tombs of ancestors, and prayers were offered to them.[3]

---

1. L. Magesa, *Anatomy of Inculturation: Transforming the Church in Africa* (Maryknoll, NY: Orbis, 2004), 112.
2. John Lukwata, *Integrated African Liturgy*, 8–9.
3. See F. X. Kyewalyanga for more information on pilgrimages to tombs of ancestors, prayers, invocations, appeals to ancestors, sacrifices, offerings, libations to ancestors, veneration of ancestors

> Many Baganda continue to believe in their ancestors even when they convert to a new religion like Christianity. . . . It is their ancestors (benevolent) who keep them from death, diseases, accidents and show interest in what they do and even make them succeed in their endeavours. God may be there, but He is not as close to them as the ancestors, whom they can turn to whenever there is a crisis.[4]

In interacting with the Ganda, one is immediately struck by the high level of consciousness and awareness of the ancestors. Every Ganda is believed to live under their watchful eye. At church festivals when food is being served, if some of it accidently drops on the floor, it is not uncommon to hear someone say "that is for the ancestors" or "the ancestors are hungry".

It is thus impossible to ignore the whole realm of ancestral spirituality that so dominates the African worldview. But where does one begin when discussing it? As always, the best place to begin is with Scripture.

Acknowledging the Ancestors

In chapter 11 of the Epistle to the Hebrews, the author gives a long list of both famous and unknown champions of the faith, all of whom were the ancestors of the Jewish Christians to whom he was writing. He reminds his readers that they are surrounded by a "great cloud of witnesses" and exhorts them to remember this and be encouraged by it as they press on in the faith (Heb 12:1). These faithful departed ancestors are still in some way in fellowship with the living, providing inspiration and encouragement to the church.[5] Their heroism in the face of adversity and opposition to their faith in Yahweh should inspire the living and challenge them not to give up. The examples of these heroes of faith

---

(*African Traditional Religion, Custom, and Christianity in Uganda*, [Freiburg: Offsetdruckerei, 1976], 122–123, 275–276, 280, 281, 283, 285, 288).

4. Francis Xavier Mulambuzi, "Beliefs in Ancestral Spirits: Interpreting Contemporary Attitudes of the Baganda to the Ancestors", Unpublished Master of Arts dissertation, Department of Religious Studies (University of Natal, 1997), 75–76.

5. For further discussions on this see Edison Muhindo Kalengyo, "'Cloud of Witnesses' in Hebrews 12:1 and Ganda Ancestors: An Incarnational Reflection", *Neotestamentica* 43, no. 1 (2009): 49–68.

should encourage them on their journey of faith with the assurance that they too will stand firm to the end.

Given these words of Scripture, is there any reason why we cannot refer to our believing ancestors in our celebration of the Lord's Supper? The Church of the Province of Kenya does this in its Holy Communion liturgy, in which the introduction to the creed states, "We stand together with Christians throughout the centuries and throughout the world today".[6] The fourth intercessory prayer includes the words, "we heartily thank you for our faithful ancestors and all who have passed through death to new life of joy in our heavenly home". The Sanctus reads:

> *Therefore with angels, and archangels, faithful ancestors and all in heaven, we proclaim your great and glorious name, forever praising you and saying:*

The third post-communion prayer acknowledges that God is also the God of the ancestors: "O God of our ancestors, God of our people, before whose face the human generations pass away."

Similarly, the Experimental Liturgy for Archbishop Janani Luwum Theological College in Northern Uganda includes these words:

> Brothers and sisters, we who are living on earth are not the only followers of Christ; many have already left this world and are now with God. Together we make up one great family. Let us join ourselves with them . . .
>
> Apostles and evangelists (N), witnesses of the resurrection, you are with us as we celebrate this Holy Communion.
>
> You are with us. You are with us. Praise the Lord.
>
> With saints and martyrs the following is said:
>
> And you, our ancestors in the faith (N), who have served God with a good conscience, you are with us as we celebrate this Holy Communion.
>
> You are with us. You are with us. Praise the Lord.

At the meeting of the Association of Episcopal Conferences of East Africa (AMECEA) in 1969, a special liturgy for celebrating the Eucharist was drawn up. It follows the pattern of the words that would have

6. See *A Modern Service of Holy Communion* (Nairobi: Uzima Press, 1989), 18, 23, 28, 33.

been said by an elder in his offering to the ancestors according to the ancient traditions.

> Here is your food [they are addressing God]
> Here is your drink
> All of this is yours, before it is ours . . .
> We celebrate a feast,
> But it is a feast of thanksgiving,
> We thank God.
> O God, we and our ancestors
> The fathers of our people [I would suggest "fathers and mothers"]
> We thank you and we rejoice.
> This food, we will eat in your honour.
> This drink we will drink in your honour.[7]

But while it is one thing to invoke our faithful ancestors, what do we do about those who preceded them? One option that is sometimes considered is related to the two feasts of All Saints Day and All Soul's Day. The former celebrates the departed faithful, and is observed annually on November 1 by Roman Catholics, Anglicans and some other denominations. "All Souls Day", observed on November 2 mainly by Roman Catholics, commemorates all the departed. This feast was originally instituted to remember those who died baptized but without having confessed their sins and so, according to Roman Catholic doctrine, reside in purgatory. The Roman Catholic Church teaches that intercessions (prayers) by church members on earth can cleanse these departed souls and prepare them for heaven. But there is no biblical basis for this kind of teaching.

Invoking the Ancestors

Within the Roman Catholic Church, there are those who draw a parallel between African ancestors and Christian saints, particularly as regards their role as mediators. This explains why some liturgies not only give the ancestors prominence as part of the community of the living but also

7. Lumbala, *Celebrating Jesus in Africa*, 33.

imply that they are in position to help them. For example, a eucharistic prayer based on a Kikuyu prayer reads in part:

> We beseech you,
> And in this we are in harmony
> With the spirits of our ancestors;
> We ask you to send the Spirit of life
> To bless and sanctify our offerings,
> That they may become for us the Body and Blood
> Of Jesus, our Brother and your Son.[8]

Some prayers are even more explicit in invoking the aid of the ancestors. For example, a Tanzanian eucharistic prayer based on a Luguru prayer begins by entreating God the Father for mercy, and then continues thus:

> Also you, our Grandparents
> Who sleep in the place of light,
> All ancestors, men and women, great and small,
> Help us, have compassion on us,
> So that we can also sleep peacefully.[9]

But this presentation of the ancestors as mediators with God is both theologically and culturally flawed. In traditional African thinking, the ancestors are not mediators like the Catholic saints; they are "perceived to have more power and more direct influence on the living than are the saints in Catholicism".[10] For example, the Ganda pantheon of deities (*balubaale* and all ancestral spirits) were never thought of as mediators acting on behalf of the Supreme Being. Sacrifices made to the ancestors were offered to them in their own right as beings capable of responding independently to the prayers and petitions of the living. We need to exercise caution that we do not deify the ancestors when we include them in our eucharistic prayers.

---

8. Aylward Shorter, "Three More African Eucharistic Prayers", *African Ecclesiastical Review* (*AFER*) 15 (1973): 155.
9. Shorter, "Three More African Eucharistic Prayers", 157.
10. Magesa, *Anatomy of Inculturation*, 241.

Christ Our Ancestor

I do not think that equating the ancestors with the saints is particularly helpful; instead I would argue that in thinking about the ancestors we should begin with the incarnate Christ, who is present in all cultures. It has been said that "Christ, by virtue of his incarnation, death, resurrection and ascension into the realm of spirit-power, can rightly be designated, in African terms, as Ancestor, indeed Supreme Ancestor".[11] The functional reasons for considering Jesus as an ancestor in African Christology are as follows:

> First, Jesus Christ is the ancestor because he mediates life. Second, Jesus Christ is the ancestor because he is present among the living. Third, Jesus Christ, the ancestor, is at the same time the eldest. Fourth, Jesus Christ is the ancestor because he is the mediator between God and human beings and within human community.[12]

In the majority of African societies, it is hard to conceive of fullness of life without the ancestors, given their role and influence in the life of the living. It is thus helpful to conceive of Jesus as the Ancestor who is the unique source of the fullness of life, which he confers on all who put their trust in him (John 3:16; 10:10).[13]

However, a note of caution needs to be sounded against making a simplistic comparison between Jesus and the ancestors. The ancestral aspect and activity of "natural" African ancestors fall far below that of Jesus because the former are essentially human while Jesus is divine. As Bediako says,

> Because ancestors, even in their realm of spirit existence, remain in African understanding essentially human just like ourselves, they cannot therefore ultimately be rivals of Christ in Christian consciousness. Just as there exists a clear distinction between

11. Kwame Bediako, *Christianity in Africa: The Renewal of a Non-Western Religion* (Edinburgh: Edinburgh University Press, 1995), 217.

12. Magesa, *Anatomy of Inculturation*, 112. For a detailed discussion see Lumbala, *Celebrating Jesus in Africa*, 44–50.

13. Magesa, *Anatomy of Inculturation*, 112.

> God and divinities, so also there exists a qualitative distinction between Christ as Ancestor and natural ancestors.[14]

Seeing Christ as an Ancestor is the essence of incarnational inculturation, in which the activity of Jesus is realized in the conceptual and practical idiom of African ancestral spirituality and religiosity.[15] Thus African peoples do not need "new eyes" and a "new mind" in order to see and understand the sacrificial work of Christ. Christ is incarnate in them and they are able to see him, understand him and relate to him from the point of view of their cultures (in this case their traditional religious experience). To ask them to denounce this is to ask them to do the impossible – how on earth can one denounce or abandon himself or herself?

A Plea

Given that ancestral spirituality need not conflict with Scripture and does not undermine the status of Jesus Christ, should we not make an effort to ensure that ancestral spirituality is reflected in the eucharistic celebration to make it meaningful to the African peoples? As I have shown above, there are a number of ways in which this can be done.

14. Bediako, *Christianity in Africa*, 217–218.
15. Magesa, *Anatomy of Inculturation*, 112.

9

HEALING, PROTECTION, AND THE LORD'S SUPPER

While I was researching this book, I attended many churches and watched what was happening when the Lord's Supper was celebrated. In liturgical churches, I sometimes found it painful to sit listening to the recitation of abstract and ambiguous prayers that were often divorced from the person who was reading them. It is not that I do not like written prayers. They have their place in our shared liturgical life as well as our individual lives. But there should also be time given for individual worshippers to offer their own prayers. Too often, even when time was allowed for personal prayer, the service leader would not be silent at all or would rush in to say "Oh Lord hear our prayers" after only a few seconds of silence. I was tempted to put up my hand and say, "Please wait! I haven't had time to pray yet!"

But, some of you may ask, why are you concerned about personal prayer while the church is celebrating the Lord's Supper? Don't intercessory prayers belong in a different part of the worship service? To answer this question, let us look first at African spirituality in general and then at the theology of the Eucharist and its recognition of Christ as the supplier of all we need.

African Spirituality

African spirituality has a strongly practical bent. In some respects, it is similar to the Jewish understanding of the word *shalom*, which refers not only to peace with God but also to peace and prosperity in this world, that is, to the fullness of a blessed life. For Africans, a blessed life involves not only physical health but also increasing wealth (crops, animals, money, buildings and houses), success in business, at work, in education and even in politics, and the bearing of children and the physical and spiritual welfare of those children. Barrenness is a serious issue. Someone who does not bear children for the family or the clan is regarded as an enemy of the family, someone who is in a way killing the family or clan. So people will go to great lengths to have children. They also pray for protection against evil spirits and witchcraft, and for peace and freedom.

In African traditional religions, sacrifices would be offered to divinities and to the ancestors in hopes of achieving a blessed life. Even today, many Christians will turn to a traditional healer and ask him or her to perform some ritual for them when they are experiencing troubles. They do this rather than turning to the Lord's Supper and seeing that Christ has provided for all their needs.

Christ as the Supplier of All We Need

The writer of the Letter to the Hebrews was addressing a Christian community that was tempted to abandon the faith and revert to Judaism or some form of traditional religion. He writes to persuade the readers not to do this, and warns them of real dangers in trying to do so (Heb 3:12; 6:4–6). He emphasizes the "once for all" aspect of the sacrificial death of Christ (Heb 7:27; 9:26, 28; 10:10) – stressing that Christ's death that had taken care of their past concerns was also efficacious for their present and future concerns.

Many African Christians are in a similar position to the people to whom the author of Hebrews wrote. They do not have a strong grasp of the all-sufficiency of the eternal sacrifice of Christ, and this explains "both the continuation of demands for sacrifice and the reintroduction of such requirements today".[1] Yet the Bible clearly teachers that the blood of Christ on the cross brings salvation to all who put their faith in him. As we saw in chapter 5, his death as a covenant sacrifice signalled the establishment of a covenant relationship between Christ and his followers. It also signals the ongoing healing and protection he extends to individuals and the community. This is a point that African believers need to be reminded of again and again, each time the Lord's Supper is celebrated. The Eucharist should be seen as a celebration of healing and health, not only for individuals but also for the community.

As stated above, health in the African understanding does not only concern itself with physical health. It broadly refers to an "ontological balance between God and his people, spirits and human beings, departed and living". Any imbalance in any of these relationships will bring suffering and will require restoration through a process of healing.[2] So the *root metaphor* of healing becomes an important category applicable to the celebration of the Lord's Supper. This is necessary for harmony in the community. What people are looking for are healing, protection and blessings in their daily lives. Unfortunately, the translated eucharistic liturgies that are currently being used do not directly address these issues. They are so rooted in church tradition and Western dogmatic disputes that they are irrelevant to the people.

The Eucharist should be the focus of Christian healing in the community of faith. God's salvation in Christ aims at the wholesome healing of humanity and the world. Given that life in Africa is "eminently communitarian",

> Christ's healing process in Africa today must be eminently a communitarian reality which reaches the person in one's individual, social and cosmological levels of life experience. Consequently, the concrete local Christian community must be the regular place where Christ is experienced as the Divine Healer. If the community is the place of healing, then the Eucharist, from which the life of such community flows and in

1. William David Spencer, "Christ's Sacrifice as Apologetic: An Application of Hebrews 10:1–18", *Journal of the Evangelical Theological Society* 40, no. 2 (June 1997): 198–190.
2. See further Chukwuma J. Okoye, "A Relevant African Eucharistic Celebration", *African Ecclesiastical Review* (*AFER*) 42, no. 5–6 (2000): 239–240.

> which it finds its apex, will be the centre of the whole process of encounter between the Diviner Healer and the human being.[3]

Because of the importance of healing in African religiosity,[4] healing services are increasingly becoming an essential component of church ministry in Africa. The African Instituted Churches have put healing at the centre of ministry to the faithful. But this healing should not be sought in a vacuum, it should be closely tied to the blood of Christ on the cross, which brings salvation to all who put their faith in him and also continues to bring healing and protection. By stressing this in our celebrations of the Lord's Supper, we enhance the people's awareness that Christ is the one who offers healing and protection for individuals and the community.

Incorporating Healing in the Lord's Supper

Some communities have attempted to address the deficit of emphasis on healing in our Westernized celebration of the Lord's Supper. For example, in Kenya a eucharistic prayer based on the traditional prayers of the Meru people reads in part:

> Owner of all things
> We offer you this cup in memory of your Son.
> We beg you for life,
> For healthy people with no disease,
> May they bear healthy children,
> And also women who suffer because they are barren,
> Open the way by which they may see children.
> Give the good life to our parents and kinsmen
> Who are with you.[5]

This prayer captures an African's overriding concern for human life in very concrete terms. The requests are specific, not abstract and generalized.

3. Fernando Domingues, *Christ Our Healer: A Theological Dialogue with Aylward Shorter* (Nairobi: Pauline Publications Africa, 2000), 100–101.

4. Magesa, *Anatomy of Inculturation*, 81.

5. Shorter, "Three More African Eucharistic Prayers", 156.

Life is the fulcrum around which everything revolves and the centre from which everything flows.

An Igbo eucharistic prayer begins by acknowledging God as the creator and source of all blessings in life:

> Our Father, Father of our ancestors,
> We gather together to praise and thank you with our sacrifice.
> Your children stand before you, thanking, praising and
> rejoicing in you:
> Because you are life,
> Because you lead and protect us one by one.
> Because you give us life and cause us to increase in the world.
> Your power and glory is manifest in the heaven and the earth.
> The sun, the moon, and the stars, which fill the heavens
> proclaim Your glory.
> This goodly land in which we live, is the work of your hands.
> The food which gives us life, produce of the land, is your
> blessing.[6]

Life in its wholeness and the blessing of progeny are overriding motifs in this and many other African prayers of petition and thanksgiving.[7]

One characteristic of African prayers is that they are concrete and devoid of the abstractness that characterizes most of the written prayers in the current missionary translated liturgies. This may be one reason why people choose to go to African Instituted Churches, where prayer and petitions are more concrete and spontaneous.

Samuel Olarewaju has criticised those who seek protection, healing and the like in the blood of Christ. He writes:

> To pray and cover various objects with the blood of Christ as protection against demonic attacks, epidemics, natural disasters, accidents, and other such experiences is, in my opinion, without scriptural warrant. The practice is paralled in various traditional religions where . . . there is strong belief in the magical use of sacrificial to avert evil. Therefore, we should consider it

6. Eugene Uzukwu, "Blessing and Thanksgiving among the Igbo (Nigeria): Towards an African Eucharistic Prayer", *African Ecclesiastical Review* (*AFER*) 72 (1980): 19.
7. Uzukwu, "Food and Drink", 18.

syncretistic for Christians to ascribe the same efficacy to the blood of Christ.[8]

Healing and the Blood of Christ

Olarewaju makes a rather unhelpful academic distinction between the legitimate use of the "authority of the name of Christ" against demonic powers and the invocation of "the blood of Christ" that he calls syncretistic. A more careful interaction with the biblical texts and the religious experience of the African community he studied would have helped him arrive at a different conclusion.

The "blood of Christ" should be understood not as a substance but as his very life given in sacrifice. It points to Christ's self-giving of his life on the cross as a redeeming sacrifice for sin. That is what the Apostle Paul is referring to when he uses the phrase "through his blood" or "by his blood" (Rom 3:25; 5:9; Eph 1:7; 2:13; Col 1:20). The writer of Hebrews was well aware of the importance of blood in the sacrificial system and in relation to establishing a covenant, and stressed that Christ's blood was shed in sacrifice (Heb 9:7, 18–25; 10:19; 13:11–12).

In the Old Testament, blood is identified with life (Lev 17:11; Deut 12:23). That was why it was able to atone for sins, and hence its important role in atoning sacrifices (see Lev 4:5, 6, 7, 16–18, 25, 30, 34; 5:9; 8:15). Christ's blood should thus be understood as his incarnate and risen life, and so does offer protection, healing and the like. This is what Olarewaju has failed to appreciate.

Some may ask why these practical concerns should be included in a eucharistic prayer. Don't they belong in the intercessory prayers during the worship? True, and they are also included there. But the point I am making is that including them in the eucharistic prayer assures the faithful that the eucharistic sacrifice is being offered for their practical needs as well as for their spiritual needs.

It is rightly held that the blood of Christ on the cross brings salvation to all who put their faith in him. While this blood continues to save the

8. Samuel Olarewaju, "The Efficacy of Prayer in the Blood of Christ in Contemporary African Christianity", *Africa Journal of Evangelical Theology* 22, no. 1 (2003): 45.

believer, it also continues to bring healing and protection. The Lord's Supper must continue to hold out his offer of healing and protection for individuals and the community.

10

COMMUNION, FELLOWSHIP AND THE LORD'S SUPPER

While the Last Supper was a Passover meal, that was not all it was. For Jesus it was also a farewell meal with his closest associates during his mission here on earth. That is why he said, "I have eagerly desired to eat this Passover with you before I suffer" (Luke 22:15). His close ties with the Twelve were about to be severed by his violent death, and he particularly wanted to share this final meal with them while preparing them for what lay ahead. It would be the last time he had this type of fellowship with them. Thus the Last Supper was simultaneously a Passover meal, a farewell meal, and a fellowship meal.[1]

We should not lose sight of those last two elements as we celebrate the Lord's Supper. We are reminded of this in the Letter to the Hebrews, which stresses that one of the great benefits of the sacrificial death of Christ is fellowship and communion with God for all who have put their faith in Christ (Heb 10:19–22). But that fellowship and communion are not all that the writer speaks of – in the very next verses he exhorts the believers to gather for fellowship with one another (Heb 10:23–25). In that era, such gatherings would have involved a eucharistic celebration. Thus these verses bring out the need for hospitality when we celebrate the Lord's Supper. As Lumbala puts it, "The Eucharist is the place of communion between God and human beings, a place of communion among human beings, a place of intercession for the world".[2]

1. Marshall, *Last Supper*, 80–82.
2. Lumbala, *Celebrating Jesus in Africa*, 26.

Communion and Children

As was argued in an earlier chapter, the Lord's Supper is a place of communion not only with living believers but also with the faithful dead, whom we remember as we meet. There is a close tie here with traditional African sacrifices, which also involved whole communities. They enjoyed communion with the deity, with the ancestors, and with human beings. No one was excluded from these sacrifices. Every family or clan member participated: young and old. Likewise the benefits that accrued from such sacrifices flowed to all. Because they all participated in the sacrifice, all shared in the benefits. There was real communion and fellowship at such sacrifices.

How sad it is then that when we meet to celebrate Christ's sacrifice, some churches in Africa exclude young members of God's family from that celebration. Christ died for all; and so all members of the community of faith must share in all the benefits he bestows. Yet in the majority of Protestant churches in Africa (especially Anglican churches), the rite of confirmation is still considered a prerequisite for participation in the Lord's Supper. In most of these churches, children have to be twelve before they can be confirmed. Once they reach that age they register for a confirmation class, which involves some six to twelve months of instruction in the Christian faith. I have no doubt that such instruction is needed and valuable for the whole of our Christian journey here on earth. But should this instruction and the ritual of confirmation be so closely tied to admission to the participation in the sacrament of Holy Communion or the Eucharist?

The New Testament never mentions a rite of confirmation. Rather, it regards baptism as the sacrament of initiation into the family of God. Paul explicitly links this rite with the Old Testament practice of circumcision, saying:

> In him [Christ] also you were circumcised with a spiritual circumcision, by putting off the body of the flesh in the circumcision of Christ; when you were buried with him in baptism, you were also raised with him through faith in the power of God, who raised him from the dead. (Col 2:11–12)

In the Old Testament, circumcision marked the Jews as the covenant people of God (Gen 17:9–14, 23–27). By linking baptism to circumcision, Paul was arguing that in the new covenant, baptism has replaced circumcision. Just as circumcision ushered the Jewish people and their children into the covenant people, so the water of baptism bring believers and their children into the new family of God's people. And if all those who have been baptised are part of God's family, why are they excluded from the family meal until they reach the age of twelve or thirteen? I can find no theological reason for doing so.

There is no doubt that baptized children are members of God's family with full rights of participation in the family meal. This was most certainly the case in the early church. The phrase "breaking of bread" appears four times in the New Testament in contexts that suggest that the Lord's Supper was celebrated in homes (Luke 24:35; Acts 2:42, 46; 20:7). There would have been children in those homes, and there is no record of those children being excluded from participation in the Lord's Supper.

We would do well to remember that Jesus himself welcomed children, held them in his arms and blessed them. He was angry with those who tried to hinder children from coming to him (Mark 10:13–16). This point was brought home to me on Christmas day in 2006 when I preached and celebrated the Lord's Supper at St Stephen's Church Kisugu in the Anglican Diocese of Kampala, Uganda. As I administered the bread and wine to the communicants, one little girl came and knelt before me. She stretched out her both hands to receive the Lord's Supper. I had preached about Jesus as the Prince of Peace that morning. With a clear conscience, I administered the Lord's Supper to her fully convinced that the Lord Jesus Christ would have done the same. He who welcomed children and blessed them by laying his hands on them would not have sent away that little saint, for in Jesus's words, "for it is to such as these that the kingdom of heaven belongs" (Matt 19:14). More importantly, this baptized girl was a full member of God's New Testament covenant people with full unrestricted access to the fellowship meal of the people of God.

Later, in 2011, I found myself in Cambridge in the UK, attending a service held at Cambourne Church. This is an interdenominational church attended by Christians from the Church of England, the Baptist Union, the Methodist Church and the United Reformed Church. An

Anglican priest led the service while a Baptist minister preached and celebrated the Lord's Supper. In the service sheet was this notice:

> **On the second Sunday of the month, Holy Communion is celebrated in Cambourne Church**
>
> **Who can receive?** All who are truly seeking God and want to meet with God. If uncertain come forward and ask for a blessing.
>
> **What about children?** We are happy for children – those baptized or intending to be baptized – to share in this family meal but would expect that children have had some preparation beforehand and show some awareness of what they are doing. As a church we try and ensure regular Christian education about communion. We encourage parents to talk to their children about the sacrament. At the 11.00 service once every other month the children return from their activities to join with their parents in this celebration.
>
> **Receiving the elements: How?** The common cup has alcoholic wine; the individual goblets have grape juice.
>
> In serving our neighbour then we state what we are sharing in words such as:
>
> The body of Christ broken for you
And
The blood of Christ shed for you
>
> **Our Emphasis?** As a multi-denominational church we can vary the emphasis that the celebration takes and the manner of its distribution. We appreciate the different ways that this sacrament can be celebrated. This sacrament is centred on God's generosity and goodness. *We remember, share and celebrate honestly and reverently.*

I saw a similar welcome to all when I attended the Servant Christian Reformed Church in Grand Rapids, Michigan, USA, in January 2016. There the invitation to the Lord's Table in the liturgy stated:

> Congregation in the Lord Jesus Christ, the Lord has prepared this table for all who love and trust in Him for salvation. Anyone baptized in the name of the Triune God is now invited to come with gladness to this holy meal. Come then, for all is ready.

Here is an open welcome to all who are in Christ Jesus, including children.

I also noted with approval the use of grape juice as an alternative to communion wine. It seems that some things some denominations in Africa still held to be essential parts of Christian doctrine have long been abandoned by those who brought us the Western form of Christianity – and that without abandoning what the Scriptures teach.

Communion and the Extended Family of God

To understand what an extended family is, consider the Ganda of Uganda. Among the Ganda,

> a clan is a social group of fundamental importance in their social structure. The "clan" is based, in the first instance, on a clearly defined concept of blood relationship: one belongs to a clan generally, by right of birth. People of each clan call each other brothers and sisters. It is, however, possible under certain circumstances for an outsider to become a member of a clan.[3]

There are about fifty-two Ganda clans, all of which constitute one large extended family with the *Kabaka* (King) at the top of the social pyramid. Because the Ganda are a very hospitable people, hospitality is extended to all, even to those who come from other cultures.

Theologically, the family of God is an extended family – much like the Ganda family. But in practice this is not so. The Christian missionaries who brought the Christian gospel to the Ganda taught that it was doctrinally wrong for a Roman Catholic Muganda to share the bread and wine of the Lord's Supper with an Anglican Muganda, even if they came from the same clan or family! Twice I have witnessed the Lord's Supper being denied to a woman from the Anglican Church of Uganda who had married a man from the Roman Catholic faith – both times,

3. Kyewalyanga, *Traditional Religion*, 18–19.

this refusal took place at their wedding service. This to me is scandalous! Among the Ganda it is unthinkable that anyone should be excluded from a meal. Only someone who had killed a member of the family or clan or committed some outrageous or heinous act would be excluded, and then only if the necessary reconciliation rituals had not been performed or the blood of the deceased had not been avenged!

Similarly, in Burkina Faso, "gathering for a meal" has profound meaning. It emphasizes "the communal nature of such eating and the strong sense of inclusion of all those present in the sharing of the African meal".[4] Such sharing is a cherished value in the majority of African societies, for it is widely recognized that a meal is a symbol of friendship, love and unity. In sharing food and drink, life is shared. It is rare for people to eat alone or to exclude anybody from a meal.[5]

In the majority of cultures in Africa, hospitality is taken seriously, even to the extent of including food for unexpected visitors when preparing a meal. Turning down an invitation to share in a meal can be taken as an insult.[6] Participants in a communal meal are also always encouraged to eat more and more. To decline to eat more can be taken to mean that you do not like the food that has been served. That too could be insulting to the host. Even when you have already eaten in some other place, you cannot give that as a reason for declining to share in a meal when it is offered. In most cultures in Africa, eating together is not just about meeting a physical need but is an embodiment of friendship, love, unity and belonging.

All this is in line with an African's strong sense of community, for no African thinks of himself or herself as an individual but rather as part of a community. John Mbiti summed this up when he wrote, "I am because we are, and since we are, therefore I am".

I would argue that we should draw on the idea of a communal meal as a root metaphor in African celebrations of the Lord's Supper. Then the "Christian Community would know that in the species of bread

---

4. Priests of the Eastern Deanery, "Eucharistic Famine", 180.

5. Izunna Okonkwo, "Eucharist and the African Communalism", *African Ecclesiastical Review* (*AFER*) 52, no. 2–3 (2010): 112. Also see further Izunna Okonkwo, "The Sacrament of the Eucharist (as Koinonia) and African Sense of Communalism: Towards a Synthesis", *Journal of Theology for Southern Africa* 137 (July 2010): 98–99.

6. Cooke and Macy, *Christian Symbol and Ritual*, 107.

and wine, in the breaking of bread and in the sharing of the cup all are bonded together".[7] In the majority of African societies, "celebration is a community event; it both expresses and builds up the community".[8] Across various denominations in Africa, a lot of emphasis is put on the celebration of the Lord's Supper as a means of grace, but including the metaphor of its being a community meal would not only enhance the community spirit and sense of oneness of the participants but would also strengthen and enhance their Christian life.[9]

Yet it is common knowledge that intercommunion is still forbidden among the Ganda of different denominations. This has been a scandal in the African Christian church since the advent of Christianity in the nineteenth century – "From the African viewpoint . . . to deliberately exclude anyone from festivity – be it a worship event, a meal, or any other community activity – implies far more than the fact of exclusion itself. It implies that the excluded person is tainted, evil or an enemy".[10] Some of the religious conflicts and rivalries that have plagued Uganda since the nineteenth century have their roots in this kind of inter-Christian rivalry.[11] The truth needs to be told: "The Eucharist in Africa is yet to impact Africa's divisions along language and culture lines. The Eucharist assembly is in fact meant to be the communion of all peoples and classes; the Eucharist unites, it should never divide".[12]

The hostility to intercommunion also sustains the ethnic tensions that plague Africa. During the colonial era, missionary societies from different denominations agreed to operate in different regions of countries like Nigeria. The result has been an unhealthy overlap between tribal and denominational identities, bolstered by the refusal to eat and drink in fellowship together.

---

7. Okonkwo, *Eucharist and African Communalism*, 112–113. For a detailed discussion of root metaphors that should characterize the celebration of the Lord's Supper in Africa, see Chukwuma J. Okoye, "The Eucharist and African Culture", *African Ecclesiastical Review* (*AFER*) 34, no. 5 (1992): 275–285.

8. Okoye, "Eucharist in African Perspective", 165.

9. See also Uzukwu E. Elochukwu, "Liturgy and Inculturation: A Century of Catholic Worship in Onitisha", *African Ecclesiastical Review* (*AFER*) 29, no. 1 (February 1987): 22.

10. Magesa, *Anatomy of Inculturation*, 242.

11. Magesa, 242. Since Uganda's Independence in 1962, political alliances have been based on religious affiliations. Today the Democratic Party is largely Roman Catholic while the Uganda People's Congress is largely Protestant, despite many attempts to change this situation.

12. Okoye, "Eucharist in African Perspective", 169.

The Lord's Supper comes across to us from the New Testament writings as a uniting symbol of the church – it should establish that "we are one body" (1 Cor 10:17). It is scandalous that what the church graciously received as a uniting factor continues to be the basis for endless divisions in the body of Christ. Sometimes I wonder whether those who wield the power to make decisions that divide communities under the guise of safeguarding doctrine and tradition have any awareness of the pain they cause in African communities.

I strongly believe that one way in which the Lord's Supper can truly be meaningful to African communities is by the promotion of intercommunion. Without it, we are left with the scandal that members of the same family or clan cannot share in the celebration of the Lord's Supper if they belong to different denominations, yet they can all worship together when paying homage to traditional deities (*balubaale* and ancestral spirits).

The lived reality among almost all African peoples is inclusion and not exclusion. This is the essence of family and community. Working as a missionary among the Masai in Kenya, Vincent J. Donavan came face to face with this reality. He thought that the Masai people

> were badly confusing the meaning of the eucharist, or that of the church, or both. They already referred to the church as the *orporor*, the brotherhood. Now, from time to time, I heard them calling the eucharist *orporor sinyati*, the holy *orporor*, or the holy brotherhood. They would ask questions like this: "Next time you come, are we holding or making the holy *orporor*?"[13]

For the Masai Christians, there could not have been another way of understanding both church and the Lord's Supper. Church to them was that in which the essence of oneness and belonging was expressed – the brotherhood (and I would add *sisterhood*).

Church is a place of belonging for all. So is the Lord's Supper that is celebrated in the church. It strengthens the fellowship among us. Where church and the Lord's Supper are, there cannot be exclusion. Yet denominational exclusion at the Lord's Supper remains a regrettable scandal of the church in Africa in the twenty-first century and should be

13. Vincent J. Donovan, *Christianity Rediscovered*, 123.

abandoned as it is not African. By this I mean it does not correspond to the African ideal of celebrating life through community. In sharing in the Lord's Supper, "the worshippers demonstrate their communion not only with God and the ancestors, but also with one another. . . . for one not to share in feast is to deny this communion and poses a danger to the whole purpose of the gathering".[14]

The issue of hospitality at the Lord's Supper is therefore very important for the African expression and understanding of church as a gathering or an assembly of believers – one extended family.

14. Magesa, *Anatomy of Inculturation*, 244.

11

CONCLUSION

The focus in this book has been on the endemic famine of the Lord's Supper among his people in Africa. You see it everywhere across denominations, and particularly in the rural congregations scattered in villages across Africa. Not that urban congregations are spared the famine of the Lord's Supper; the difference is merely one of degree.

The causes of the famine range from a waning understanding and appreciation of the significance of the Lord's Supper to human restrictions on who may access the Lord's Supper that have led to the exclusion of the majority of the faithful on the continent. The undesirable consequence of this is the unfortunate division of the church in Africa into two groups: the eucharistically privileged few and the majority eucharistically underprivileged, who remain excluded from the Lord's Table. This book has addressed the current challenges encountered in the celebration of the Lord's Supper and explored possible workable solutions.

Some of the restrictions still being imposed on the African Christians by the ecclesiastical authorities have long been abandoned by those who brought them to Africa. A case in point is the continued exclusion of children from the Lord's Table by some denominations in Africa.

Any plausible discussion of the Lord's Supper must take as its starting point the New Testament itself and pay attention to the authentic meaning and significance of the Lord's Supper based on Jesus's words of institution at the Last Supper. As has been shown, that meal was a sacrificial meal, at which Christ is the only mediator and agent of sacrifice. Our liturgy and our actions when we celebrate the Lord's Supper should reflect the nature of Christ's sacrifice and what was accomplished by his death.

Our liturgy and actions should also reflect the fact that the risen Lord Jesus Christ incarnates in the various cultures to make himself known as Saviour and Lord. This is the way God has chosen to communicate his grace and mercy. His Son Jesus Christ meets and interacts with his people in their individual cultures through a process of inculturation.

Culture remains an indissoluble aspect of any group of people anywhere in the world. Without it we would not be human. No group of people can exist apart from culture. And each group of people has a particular culture. Each has unique ways of being identified as a cultural group. (It is important to remember this and to avoid speaking of Africans as a homogenous society with uniform traits.)

The need for inculturation is particularly urgent when it comes to the participatory celebration of the Lord's Supper. If this foundational ritual of the church is to be relevant to African peoples, it needs to be interpreted in ways that are meaningful to Africans in their own cultures.

A Call to Action

> The famine in Ethiopia and the Sudan has taught us that lack of food is a problem which cannot simply be solved by food-aid from outside or foreign resources. As long as subservience to economic structures and markets prevents Africans from the crops they need to feed themselves, famine in Africa will be endemic. Perhaps this is an analogy for the Eucharist. Ending the eucharistic famine in Africa demands new, local initiatives. The church has it in her power to end the famine. It is her duty to do so. But ending it demands boldness and originality and the readiness to modify recent, inessential traditions.[1]

It is within the power of the church in Africa to make decisions for the spiritual and physical welfare of her people. The word "church" is here used to refer specifically to the hierarchy and leadership of the church in Africa – the archbishops, bishops, cardinals, pastors, priests, ministers and all spiritual leaders. They owe it to the faithful in Africa to speedily

1. Shorter, "Eucharistic Famine", 136.

implement the inculturation of the Christian message in Africa, and to do it well.

There was a time when what was made in Europe and America was assumed to be good for Africa. That time has long passed. Africa should no longer be bound by decisions and policies bred in the West. Boniface Luykx has clearly demonstrated that liturgical documents crafted in the West have failed to have the desired impact on the worship lives and experience of Christians in Africa largely because of their foreign character.[2] Such materials leave believers uneasy, frustrated and confused as they do not address their spiritual needs and remain unintelligible because they are designed in a completely different cultural context.

Even church canons put in place in the West to promote inculturation in Africa contain clauses that limit inculturation.[3] This is a classic example of the proverbial saying: "giving with the right hand and taking away with the left." As Africans we know what is best for us and have all it takes to do that which serves our good.

The regrettable reality is that church decisions on African issues are by and large still made in Europe and America. Even though the majority of Christians are in the global South, the decisions that govern the church worldwide are still largely made in the global North. This is used by the West as a control measure. Africans still have to seek permission from Rome or Canterbury (and other self-serving centres of religious power) to be who they are in their Christian experience and practice, and often that permission is denied. Approval procedures can be held up for years by high authorities or machinations at the lower levels. All of this begs the question of whether African Christians are able to manage their own affairs. Why does the African church continue to allow itself to be controlled by those among whom Christianity is increasingly on the decline? Why should Africans continue to find their self-worth in the cultures of others?

The African church's blame game is no longer viable. To continue to blame inaction on the missionaries is to escape responsibility. The church in Africa must now begin to be accountable to her people. It is within

2. Boniface Luykx, "The Impact of the Liturgical Documents", *African Ecclesiastical Review* (*AFER*) 13, no. 2 (1971): 100–104.
3. Gerard Nwagwu, "A Canonical Perspective of Liturgical Inculturation in Africa", *African Ecclesiastical Review* (*AFER*) 43, no. 1–2 (2001): 60–61.

the power of the African church to change and abandon that which does not aid church growth and ministry in Africa.

A Call to Dialogue

For the continued presence and growth of faith in Christ Jesus in Africa, it is imperative that a dialogue continues between the revealed risen Christ and the lived realities of the socio-cultural groups in Africa. This dialogue should not be hindered by selfish ecclesiastical powers. Constant conversation or dialogue between faith in Christ and the cultures of the various socio-cultural groups in Africa is the only way to keep the faith in Christ as experienced by Africans deeply rooted in Africa.

A case has been made that this conversation and dialogue needs to take cognisance of the burden of Africa's particular history in regard to slavery and colonialism. These twin evils continue to affect us psychologically and socially. Slavery "desecrated much of Africa by diminishing the humanity of Africans in various aspects". Meanwhile, missionaries "vilified African religiosity". They totally disregarded all evidence of "the divine self-revelation in the cultures in Africa".[4] Yet while I acknowledge the need to be aware of our history, we must guard against the real danger and temptation of being trapped in it. We should not allow ourselves to be held captive by our history. While it is permissible to lament, after lamentation we must re-engage and move on.

There are multiple ramifications of a meaningful dialogue between the revelation of Jesus Christ and the various socio-cultural groups in Africa. Two important practical requirements for "decoding the Will of God" by bringing the Scriptures and African cultures and religiosity into conversation have been suggested:[5]

> First, there is need to continue studying intensely and seriously the biblical text in order to identify the necessary cultural expressions that surround the Divine Will embedded there.

4. Magesa, "Christian Faith and African Culture", 2.

5. Magesa, 4. Magesa speaks of "the Will of God" rather than "the popularly used description of faith in Christ as 'Christianity'". To him, Christianity "is a loaded term since all forms of 'Christianity' are culturally conditioned and there is no such a thing as 'universal Christianity'".

> This will help us avoid as much as possible the simplistic and literalistic approaches to the Scriptures that are often characterized by the phrase "the Bible says . . . Second, and equally important, theological education must assist African pastors as well as the general faithful to revisit in unprejudiced way African indigenous religiosity so as also to discover the Divine Will in it, one that is compatible with that revealed by Christ in the New Testament. When these processes maturely merge through the practice of cultural critique of both the Bible and African Religion, we will be engaging in a proper dialogue between the Christian Faith and culture.[6]

These two processes lead in the same direction with one ultimate goal: continuous dialogue between the Christian tradition and the socio-cultural groups in Africa. The Christian tradition must of necessity dialogue with the various African cultures. The point has already been emphasized in this book and I will repeat it here: "there is no form of Christianity that can be viable if it is not incarnated or contextualized in particular cultures" – period. This is another way of saying: nothing less, nothing more; take it or leave it. There is no middle path. The Lord's Supper has to be contextualized in ways pointed out in this book for it to impact the lives of the faithful and allow for the gospel to become deeply rooted in Africa. Ultimately this, and not ecclesiastical structures and endless legislation, will guarantee the future of a strong church in Africa.

A Call to Difference

The eucharistic famine in Africa requires urgent action. The time to act was yesterday. There can no longer be room for waiting. Posterity will judge the church of today harshly for its inaction. Indecision and inaction are not strengths but weaknesses. The task before the church in Africa is not insurmountable. It is a necessary and possible task that requires swift action if the endemic famine of the Lord's Supper is to be addressed and God's people are to find relief. Then they can share in the joy of a fulfilled Christian experience through unrestricted and yet orderly access

6. Magesa, 4.

to the Lord's Supper.

All this will certainly make the African church different – a difference for the good of all. The African church remains a member and part of the universal body of Christ (his universal church) made of different parts (1 Cor 12). Uniformity is never an attribute of God. Our God is a God of variety, and as Africans we have a right to be different and to do things differently within the same body of Christ, his church, to the glory and honour of our eternal and creator God.

Magesa acknowledges that such an action will require

> formed theologians who combine the skills of artisanship, inquisitiveness and prophecy. Theologians who are trained to see fresh meaning behind what may at first sight appear to be a given in the Bible and African religiosity; theologians who possess the charism of inquisitiveness, inspiring questions that go beyond providing mere platitudes about God, who is ineffable; theologians with a prophetic vision to challenge established but non-Christic views, teachings, and structures, rather than fearful conformists or careerists interested mainly in positions in the church.[7]

Needless to say, theologians such as those may sometimes destabilize the conventional system, attracting all sorts of reactions (largely unpleasant) from the establishment. But we take comfort in knowing that Jesus Christ the "pioneer and perfecter of our faith" (Heb 12:2) aroused similar reactions. This may be the only way towards the much needed transformation that will end the eucharistic famine among God's people in Africa.

Not surprisingly, there will be frustration with the slow pace in both the acceptance and implementation of the measures suggested in this book. Some well-intentioned campaigners in the fight against endemic eucharistic famine in Africa have already voiced their frustrations:

> In Nigeria, the Roman Catholic clergy shies away from a courageous rooting of Christian life into ethnic experience. Despite hundreds of theses, both published and unpublished, that explore ways in which Christianity should be practiced in

7. Magesa, 5.

> Nigeria, the Nigerian hierarchy feels more at ease with promoting "orthodox doctrine and approved liturgical discipline". . . . very little has been done apart from translating Latin Liturgical texts and permitting dancing during the offertory procession. . . . Official Roman theology favours a situation whereby the gospel transforms and uplifts culture. The model is still evolutionist (colonialist-missionary). The gospel is always carried and communicated through a given culture – in this case, West European culture . . . Furthermore, there seems to be a lack of appreciation of how the gospel becomes different as it is being shaped by questions posed to it by the context and shaped by responding to the context in which it is received and how it remains the same, retaining its universal character.[8]

Many others (known and unknown) have set themselves on the right path to end the endemic eucharistic famine among the African peoples. I feel greatly privileged and humbled to be numbered among them through this book. The key is not to give up on the good already being done, however little. A great harvest awaits all who will bear the frustrations, hardships and the great toil, if they do not give up (Gal 6:9).The constant call of Scripture is: *Do not give up! Keep your eyes on the finish line! Finish the race!* (1 Cor 9:24–27; Phil 3:13–14; 2 Tim 4:7; Heb 12:1–2). Quitting is not and will never be an option.

The ultimate goal is the end of the endemic famine of the Lord's Supper in Africa by overcoming current challenges pointed out in this book. Noticeable adaptation has already been recorded and should be celebrated: the use of local languages in the majority of African communities, the use of African music with African musical instruments, hand-clapping and various forms of dance, etc. What needs to be progressively and practically addressed is "re-interpreting the eucharistic celebration and its structure in African terms"[9] using the culture (the rituals and symbols) of specific socio-cultural groups as explained in this book. That goal shall be achieved as we remain focused on Jesus

8. E. E. Uzukwu. "Inculturation and the Liturgy (Eucharist)", in *Paths of African Theology*, ed. Rosino Gibellini (Maryknoll, NY: Orbis, 1994), 95, 97–98.

9. Ukpong, "Inculturation: A Major Challenge to the Church in Africa Today", 260.

Christ – committed to serving and glorifying God in all that we are and do as Africans.

The church in Africa is widely acclaimed as a growing and mature church, and rightly so. But with maturity comes responsibility to make decisions now that secure the future.

The exhortation in this work is for us all to continue to fan the ongoing work of inculturation in both academia and among the faithful where it is lived out. Inculturation is both our goal and our responsibility. Christian expression cannot be left to one section of the faithful. No one is to be left out and no one's participation and contribution is to be elevated above that of others. The guiding principle is that we are in this together as God's people. We need to act together and move together. Inculturation is already happening; it is ongoing and requires the participation and contribution of each one of the faithful.

APPENDIX

THE HISTORY AND THEOLOGY OF THE LORD'S SUPPER

Over the centuries, there have been many controversies relating to the theology of the Lord's Supper. Here, I will merely summarize these, and will not delve into christological debates or claim to present solutions to the issues relating to the history and theology of the Lord's Supper.

From the Middle Ages to the sixteenth century, the Roman Catholic understanding of the Lord's Supper was unchallenged in the Western church. Key elements were the eucharistic presence and the eucharistic sacrifice. The Roman Catholic idea of the eucharistic presence is rooted in the doctrine of transubstantiation, which holds that when the priest says the prayer of consecration, the substance of the bread and wine is transformed into the substance of the body and blood of Christ. The elements may continue to look like bread and wine, but their appearance does not reflect their true substance. Closely related to this idea is the idea that the Eucharist is a propitiatory sacrifice – the same sacrifice Christ offered on the cross. This eucharistic sacrifice is regarded as being offered for the sins of both the living and the dead.

These two elements were also at the heart of the debates on eucharistic theology at the time of the Reformation in the sixteenth century. Martin Luther and other Reformers argued strongly that people are saved by "faith alone, grace alone and scripture alone". This then became the theological basis for Luther's rejection of the sacrificial character of the Mass.[1] He recognized that ascribing any "objective mediating function

1. For an outline of the doctrine of the eucharistic sacrifice at the time of the reformation see further

to the sacraments" would create a space for those who served the sacraments to introduce human mediation between God and sinners.[2] He insisted that it was the "faith of the believer that gave any power to the sacraments" and that the purpose of the Eucharist was to arouse the faith of the believer in the forgiveness of sins.[3]

Luther was also opposed to the special position of the priest in the celebration and sharing of the Eucharist. He taught that since all believers are priests (1 Peter 2:9), the priest should not have a distinctively sacrificial role. This meant that all should be able to drink the wine at the Lord's Supper, and not merely the presiding priest.

While Luther rejected the doctrine of transubstantiation, which he attributed to Aquinas, he still acknowledged the "real presence of Christ" in the Lord's Supper, but defined the mechanism as "consubstantiation", meaning that the substance of the bread and wine coexists with the body and blood of Christ in the Eucharist.[4] "There is no change in substance; the substance of both bread and the body of Christ are present together . . . The crucial point was that Christ was really present at the Eucharist – not some particular theory as to how he was present" as this would be an attempt to rationalize a mystery.[5]

Zwingli disagreed with Luther. He was unequivocal: "the Eucharist is a memorial of the suffering of Christ and not a sacrifice".[6] He rejected the literal understanding of the words of institution ("this is my body") and argued that these words are to be interpreted symbolically or figuratively. He believed that Christ was present at the Lord's Supper only symbolically or figuratively, not as a real presence.[7]

Francis S. J. Clark, *Eucharistic Sacrifice and the Reformation* (London: Darton, Longman & Todd, 1960), 93–95. See also C. W. Dugmore, "The Eucharist in the Reformation Era", in *Eucharistic Theology Then and Now*, SPCK Theological Collections 9 (London: SPCK, 1968), 59–75.

2. M. Joseph Powers, *Eucharistic Theology* (New York: Herder & Herder, 1967), 33–34. Luther was highly critical of those who earned their living by celebrating mass in the chantries often referring to them in a derogatory manner as "fat bellies".

3. Powers, *Eucharistic Theology*, 32. Compare Romans 1:17; Habakkuk 2:4 where the emphasis is "the one who is righteous will live by faith".

4. Powers (*Eucharistic Theology*, 32) further states: "For Luther, Christ is present only at the moment of the consecration, when the passion is preached and commemorated, and at the moment of communion, when the death of the Lord is proclaimed and commemorated. The presence of Christ in the eucharist does not endure beyond these moments."

5. Alister McGrath, *Historical Theology* (Oxford: Blackwell, 1998), 197.

6. McGrath, 198.

7. McGrath, 198–199; Powers, *Eucharistic Theology*, 35.

John Calvin sought to tread a middle way between the positions of Martin Luther and Zwingli. He argued that there is a close link between a symbol and what it symbolizes, making it possible and to move backwards and forwards from one to the other. Calvin's position, as quoted by McGrath, is as follows:

> Believers ought always to live by this rule: whenever they see symbols appointed by the Lord, to think and be convinced that the truth of the thing signified is surely present there. For why should the Lord put in your hands the symbol of his body, unless it was to assure you that you really participate in it? And if it is true that a visible sign is given to us to seal the gift of an invisible thing, when we have received the symbol of the body, let us rest assured that the body itself is also given to us. I therefore say . . . that the sacred mystery of the Lord's Supper consists in two things: physical signs, which, when placed in front of our eyes, represent to us (according to our feeble capacity) invisible things; and spiritual truth, which is at the same time represented and displayed through the symbols themselves.[8]

It seems fair to say that in spite of their differences as regards the nature of eucharistic presence, the Reformers all agreed on the non-sacrificial character of the Eucharist, meaning that they did not see it as a propitiatory sacrifice.

The Council of Trent's response sought to address the trio of issues regarding the Eucharist (real presence, communion, and sacrifice) in one balanced statement. Powers has summarized the response, and his words are worth quoting in full:

> The description of the Last Supper places the sacrificial character of the Eucharist in the fact that Jesus gave His body and blood to His disciples to eat and drink under the appearances of bread and wine. His command "Do this in commemoration of me" is the gift of the Eucharist and, at the same time, the constitution of a new priesthood and of an eternal sacrifice. The celebration of the old Passover leads to the gift of a new Passover, which is

8. McGrath, *Historical Theology*, 199.

> the commemoration of man's redemption in Jesus' return to the Father. Here is an integrated statement of the fact that it is in eating and drinking that Christ's sacrifice is renewed and commemorated sacramentally and the fruits of that sacrifice are granted to the believer.[9]

In this book I have argued that based on the fact that the feast at which Jesus instituted the Lord's Supper was essentially a Passover feast for which the Passover lamb was sacrificed, there is a sense in which the Lord's Supper can be understood as a sacrifice. Paul can even boldly say, "For our paschal lamb, Christ, has been sacrificed" (1 Cor 5:7). Thus the Christian sacrament of the Lord's Supper is one key tradition of the church where the understanding of Christ's death as sacrifice is celebrated.

Biblical Background to the Lord's Supper

Although Paul's words in 1 Corinthians 10 constitute the earliest account of the Lord's Supper in the New Testament, any meaningful historical and theological inquiry into the Lord's Supper must begin with the events of the Last Supper – what Jesus did and said on that occasion as recorded in the Synoptic Gospels (Matthew, Mark and Luke).

The Last Supper was "the final meal Jesus shared with his disciples before he died", while the Lord's Supper is "the community re-enactment of that meal after Jesus's death and resurrection".[10] While Christian churches disagree on how the Lord's Supper is to be interpreted, they seem to be unanimous at least on one point: that the Lord's Supper is connected with the Last Supper.[11] It is also generally accepted by scholars that the Jewish annual festival of the Passover "provides the most obvious

---

9. Powers, *Eucharistic Theology*, 41–42. For a more comprehensive answer by the Council of Trent to the accusations of the Reformers regarding the celebration of Mass, see N. David Power, *The Sacrifice We Offer: The Tridentine Dogma and Its Reinterpretations* (Edinburgh: T & T Clark, 1987), 50–93. Essentially, Trent reaffirmed that the mass was a propitiatory sacrifice, arguing that since the mass was a representation of the sacrifice of the cross, it should itself be termed a sacrifice of propitiation.

10. Kodell, *The Eucharist*, 22.

11. Kodell, 12. See further, Higgins, *The Lord's Supper*, 9; Robert J. Daly, *Christian Sacrifice*, 499.

background for the Last Supper of Jesus and his disciples".[12] The details of this Jewish celebration are set out in the section on Inculturation and the Last Supper in chapter 4 of this book.

New Testament accounts of the Last Supper and Lord's Supper

It seems reasonable to say that Jesus had a historical meal (the Last Supper) with a group of his disciples (the twelve apostles to be precise) before his death.[13] However, differences of opinion abound in discussions of the details of what took place at that historical meal. These, together with questions about the nature and meaning of the Last Supper, continue to dominate the agenda of current theological debate and reflection on this issue.[14] However, it is not the primary focus of this book to engage with the various opinions in the ongoing scholarly discussions concerning the Last Supper and the Lord's Supper.[15]

I will now examine the New Testament accounts of the Last Supper. I share Marshall's view that in the absence of "any serious historical doubts about the historicity of the Last Supper, its character and its exemplary significance", the meal Jesus had with the twelve should be our starting point.[16] But given that the earliest record of this historical meal is found in Paul's first letter to the Corinthians in the context of church life, it seems advisable to start with the church's re-enactment of the events of the Last Supper in what came to be celebrated as the Lord's Supper in the early church.

The Pauline account

Chronologically, Paul offers us the earliest description of the Last Supper in his first letter to the believers in Corinth.[17] Here we have evidence of the celebration of the Lord's Supper as it came to be known in the early church (1 Cor 11:23–25). It is clear from the preceding verses (1 Cor

12. Marshall, *Last Supper*, 23; Higgins, *The Lord's Supper*, 13, 45, 51; Eduard Schweizer, *The Lord's Supper*, 32, while acknowledging an inherent relationship between the Last Supper and the Passover tradition, does not take it to mean that the two are necessarily or obviously linked.

13. Marshall, *Last Supper*, 31.

14. Marshall, 31.

15. For a detailed study of the various scholarly opinions regarding the Last Supper and the Lord's Supper, see Kodell, *The Eucharist*, 22–37; Marshall, *Last Supper*, 30–31, 36–41.

16. See further Marshall, *Last Supper*, 30–31.

17. Marshall, 31–32.

11:17–22), that there were abuses in the celebration of the Lord's Supper that Paul seeks to correct through the instruction in this letter. Evidence within the text further shows that Paul is quoting existing tradition: "For I received from the Lord what I also handed on to you" (1 Cor 11:23).[18] The passage also implies that Paul had previously passed on this tradition to them (possibly when he founded the Corinthian church in around AD 51). If this reconstruction is true (and there is no substantial reason to doubt it), then "this means that Paul's statement was in existence within some twenty years of the death of Jesus".[19]

Of greater relevance to our discussion are Paul's words in 1 Corinthians 10:16–18 quoted in full below:

> The cup of blessing that we bless, is it not a sharing in the blood of Christ? The bread that we break, is it not a sharing in the body of Christ? Because there is one bread, we who are many are one body, for we all partake of the one bread. Consider the people of Israel; are those who eat the sacrifices partners in the altar?

The phrase "blood of Christ" here refers to his life sacrificially given up in death. The sacrificial meaning of the "cup" and "bread" will become clearer when later in this appendix we examine the cup and bread sayings of Jesus at the celebration of the Last Supper in the Synoptic Gospels (Matthew, Mark and Luke).

Commenting on 1 Corinthians 10:16–18, Kwesi A. Dickson writes: "What Paul is saying here is that eating and drinking at the Lord's Table is sharing in the death of Christ, and also sharing in life with the other".[20] It will be demonstrated in this appendix that the Eucharist (which is the participatory celebration of the sacrificial death of Christ) brings the

---

18. As observed by Marshall, *Last Supper*, 32, the words and vocabulary used in this section are not commonly found in Paul's writing, strengthening the evidence that Paul is quoting an existing tradition. Marshall also argues that the phrase "I received from the Lord" is not to be understood in the sense of some special divine revelation to Paul; "rather he is referring to tradition that was current in the Church and which ultimately came from the Lord himself". There are three possible places from which Paul could have got this tradition: Antioch, Damascus, and Jerusalem (see Marshall, *Last Supper*, 32–33).

19. Marshall, *Last Supper*, 32.

20. Kwesi A. Dickson, *Theology in Africa* (London: Darton, Longman & Todd, 1984), 196.

faithful into an intimate relationship with the risen Lord Jesus Christ and with one another.

The Synoptic Gospels' account of the Last Supper

The Gospels of Matthew, Mark and Luke all describe Jesus's final meal with the twelve apostles. The accounts in Matthew 26:26–28 and Mark 14:22–25 are so similar that it has been generally accepted that Matthew's account is simply a modified version of Mark's, and in this discussion they will be taken together.[21] Luke's narrative (Luke 22:14–20) is distinctive in its details and emphases. In many ways it is similar to the account Paul gives in 1 Corinthians (1 Cor 11:23–26), and so Luke and Paul's accounts are often considered together. John's Gospel says nothing about the institution of the Lord's Supper at the Supper. Instead it gives us the unique story about Jesus washing the disciples' feet (John 13). But implicit eucharistic teaching can be discerned in the bread of life discourse in John 6:35–58 (note especially verses 51–58). In John the death of Jesus coincides with the slaughter of the Passover lambs, probably to underscore his point that Jesus is the "lamb of God who takes away the sin of the world" (John 1:29). For John, the Supper takes place the previous night before the Passover lambs are slaughtered (a day earlier than in the Synoptics). While John relates the death of Jesus to the Passover, I will argue that in John the Last Supper is not a Passover meal.

Marshall and Kodell have examined the differences and similarities in the Synoptic narratives of the Last Supper and the section that follows is largely dependent on their work.[22]

The significant differences between Mark / Matthew and Luke can be summed up as follows: Mark / Matthew records Jesus instructing the apostles to "Take (and eat)" which is absent in Luke. Luke's account shows that the cup was shared "after the supper" and records Jesus's words over the cup as "the new covenant in my blood" whereas in Mark / Matthew we have "This is my blood of the new covenant". Jesus's authorization of the apostles to repeat what he had done is conspicuously absent in Mark / Matthew, while in Luke we have Jesus telling the apostles, "Do this in remembrance of me".

---

21. See Marshall, *Last Supper*, 33, 161, note 11 for details.
22. For details see Kodell, *The Eucharist*, 19–21; Marshall, *Last Supper*, 33–56.

There are also similarities between the different accounts. They all agree that the Last Supper took place the night before Jesus died – or as other authors have said, "in the shadow of Jesus's death".[23] The Synoptic Gospels insist that the last meal Jesus had with the apostles 'was a Passover meal, taking place on the first evening of the Passover, while the lambs are being slaughtered in the temple".[24] Mark / Matthew and Luke all use the word "covenant" with respect to the cup, and it is clear that Mark / Matthew have in mind the sprinkling of the blood of the Sinai covenant on the people (Exod 24:5–8). Luke, on the other hand quotes Jesus as speaking of the cup as a "new covenant in my blood", suggesting that Luke is making a link between Jesus's actions and Jeremiah's prophecy about the new covenant (Jer 31:31–34).[25]

Eschatological overtones are also reflected in the Last Supper. Implied in the accounts of the Synoptic Gospels is the important theme of the fulfilment of the kingdom of God. For Paul, however, the eschatological links with the Last Supper are in terms of the *parousia* – the second coming of the Lord Jesus Christ. Thus Paul writes, "For as often as you eat this bread and drink this cup, you proclaim the Lord's death until he comes" (1 Cor 11:26).

Kodell's summary of the Synoptic narratives of the Last Supper warrants being quoted in full:

> At a festive meal on the eve of his death, which may have been a Passover meal, Jesus gave a new interpretation to a familiar Jewish family and social ritual. During the main course of the meal, acting as the host or as the *paterfamilias* he said a blessing over the bread, broke it, and passed it to his friends, saying, "This is my body". After the main meal, he held a cup of wine (the third or fourth in a Paschal meal), blessed it as he had the

23. Edward Ratcliff, "The Holy Communion: Its Beginnings and Early Development", in David Cairns et al., *The Holy Communion* (London: SCM, 1947), 19.

24. Kodell, *The Eucharist*, 19.

25. The comparison made here is not exhaustive. As Kodell (*The Eucharist*, 20) has observed, the situation regarding "exactly what Jesus did (*ipsissima facta*) and said (*ipsissima verba*)" at the Last Supper is more complicated than this. For example, was there one cup as in Mark / Matthew or two as in Luke's account? Did the apostles drink before the words of institution as in Mark (14:23–24) or afterwards? Did Jesus say his blood was being poured out "for many" (Mark / Matthew) or "for you" (as in Luke)? To try to address these issues here would be to deviate from the primary focus of this book.

bread, and gave it to the rest with words identifying the wine as his blood. The disciples understood that Jesus was sharing himself with them in an intimate way through this gesture. The convictions which appear in the Supper narratives include the understanding that Jesus is foretelling his death, a death which will bring forgiveness of sins; that he is inaugurating a new covenant, that this meal is a harbinger of the banquet in the kingdom, and that he is giving them something to imitate.[26]

Conclusion

In this appendix, I have outlined some of the history and theology of the Lord's Supper and have dealt with the New Testament accounts of that supper. I have shown here and in the rest of the book that on balance, the available evidence indicates that the Last Supper (the last meal that Jesus had with his disciples) was a Passover meal.

In the early church, the emphasis was on the community celebration of the Lord's Supper. However, during the medieval period the celebration of the Lord's Supper came to be considered a clerical preserve. The community of the faithful were forced to withdraw to the periphery and were reduced almost to spectators instead of participants in the celebration of the eucharistic sacrifice. The abuses of the Lord's Supper during this period, coupled with the theological extremity of the doctrine of transubstantiation and the understanding of the Eucharist as a propitiatory sacrifice for both the living and the dead, were among the sparks that flared up at the time of the Reformation.

The Reformers while differing in their theology of the Lord's Supper, were all agreed that the Eucharist was not a sacrifice. The major theological and institutional divide into Roman Catholics and Protestants that began at that time has remained, with each group espousing its eucharistic theology in a rather uncompromising manner. It is worth noting that the missionary churches (exemplified by the Roman Catholic and Anglican churches in Uganda) have continued to reflect this division in both their understanding and celebration of the Lord's Supper. It seems right to say

26. Kodell, *The Eucharist*, 21.

that though Vatican II changed some of this in the rest of the world, it has had little impact in Africa, not least in present-day Uganda.

Yet it is time for this division to start to break down, and one of the key elements that may contribute to this is a better understanding of the sacrificial nature of the Eucharist. This is something that will indeed speak to African hearts, given the African traditional understandings of the centrality of sacrifice (a topic that has been addressed in chapter 5 of this book).

BIBLIOGRAPHY

Published Books and Journal Articles

Anagwo, C. Emmanuel. "Christianity and the African Culture: Integrating the Vision of Liturgical Inculturation". *African Ecclesiastical Review* (*AFER*) 56, no. 4 (2014): 276–299.

Barclay, William. *The Lord's Supper*. London: SCM, 1967.

Beckwith, R. T. and J. E. Tiller, eds., *Holy Communion and Its Revision*. Latimer Monographs III. Appleford: Marcham Manor Press, 1972.

Bediako, Kwame. *Christianity in Africa: The Renewal of a Non-Western Religion*. Edinburgh: Edinburgh University Press, 1995.

Bolt, Peter et al., *The Lord's Supper in Human Hands: Who Should Administer*. Camperdown: Australian Church Record, 2008.

———. *The Lord's Supper in Human Hands: Epilogue*. Camperdown: Australian Church Record, 2010.

Carson, D. A. *Christ and Culture Revisited*. Grand Rapids, MI: Eerdmans, 2008.

Chase, Nathan Peter. "A History and Analysis of the Missel Romain les Dioceses du Zaire". *Obscula* 6, no. 1 (2013): 28–36. Online at http://digitalcommons.csbsju.edu/obsculta/vol6/iss1/14.

Chibuko, C. Patrick. "A Practical Approach to Liturgical Inculturation". *African Ecclesiastical Review* (*AFER*) 43, no. 1–2 (2001): 2–27.

Chilton, Bruce. *Jesus' Prayer and Jesus' Eucharist: His Personal Practice of Spirituality*. Valley Forge, PA: Trinity Press International, 1997.

Chupungco, A. J. *Cultural Adaptation of the Liturgy*. New York: Paulist, 1982.

Clark, S. J. Francis. *Eucharistic Sacrifice and the Reformation*. London: Darton, Longman & Todd, 1960.

Cooke, Bernard, and Gary Macy. *Christian Symbol and Ritual: An Introduction*. Oxford: Oxford University Press, 2005.

da Silva, Jose Antunes. "Bread and Wine for the Eucharist: Are They Negotiable?" *African Ecclesiastical Review* (*AFER*) 34, no. 5 (1992): 258–271.

Daly, J. Robert. *Christian Sacrifice: The Judaeo-Christian Background before Origen*. Washington DC: Catholic University of America Press, 1978.

———. *The Origins of the Christian Doctrine of Sacrifice*. London: Darton, Longman & Todd, 1978.

Davies, Horton. *Bread of Life and Cup of Joy: Newer Ecumenical Perspectives on the Eucharist*. Grand Rapids, MI: Eerdmans, 1993.

Dickson, Kwesi, A. *Theology in Africa*. London: Darton, Longman & Todd, 1984.

Domingues, Fernando. *Christ Our Healer: A Theological Dialogue with Aylward Shorter*. Nairobi: Pauline Publications Africa, 2000.

Donovan, J. Vincent. *Christianity Rediscovered: An Epistle from the Masai*. London: SCM, 1978, 1982.

Dugmore, C. W. "The Eucharist in the Reformation Era". In *Eucharistic Theology Then and Now*, 59–75. SPCK Theological Collections 9. London: SPCK, 1968.

Edwards, Don. "Christ and Culture: Some Preliminary Reflections". *Colloquium* 28, no. 2 (1996): 82–95.

Ganly, John C. "The Eucharistic Famine in Africa". *African Ecclesiastical Review* (*AFER*) 27, no. 5 (1985): 302–303.

Gibson, Paul. "Forum: Eucharistic Food – May We Substitute?" *Worship* 76, no. 5 (September 2002): 445–455.

Hearne, B. "Christology and Inculturation". *African Ecclesiastical Review* (*AFER*) 22 (1980): 335–341.

Heron, Alasdair. *Table and Tradition: Towards an Ecumenical Understanding of the Eucharist*. Edinburgh: Handsel Press, 1983.

Higgins, A. J. B. *The Lord's Supper in the New Testament*. London: SCM, 1952.

Jeremias, J. *The Eucharistic Words of Jesus*, 2nd ed. Translated by Arnold Ehrhardt. Oxford: Basil Blackwell, 1955.

Kalengyo, M. Edison. "The Sacrifice of Christ and Ganda Sacrifice: A Contextual Interpretation in Relation to the Eucharist". In *The Epistle to the Hebrews and Christian Theology*, edited by R. J. Bauckham, D. R. Driver, T. A. Hart and N. MacDonald, 302–318. Grand Rapids, MI: Eerdmans, 2009.

———. *Sacrifice in Hebrews and the Pauline Epistles*. Nairobi: Acton, 2015.

———. "'Cloud of Witnesses' in Hebrews 12:1 and Ganda Ancestors: An Incarnational Reflection". *Neotestamentica* 43, no. 1 (2009): 49–68.

Klaus, Fiedler. *Christianity and African Culture: Conservative German Protestant Missionaries in Tanzania 1900–1940*. Leiden: Brill, 1996.

Kodell, Jerome. *The Eucharist in the New Testament*. Collegeville, MN: Liturgical Press, 1988.

Kraft, H. Charles. *Christianity in Culture: A Study in Dynamic Biblical Theologizing in Cross-Cultural Perspective*. Maryknoll, NY: Orbis, 1979.

Kyewalyanga, F. X. *African Traditional Religion, Custom, and Christianity in Uganda*. Freiburg: Offsetdruckerei, 1976.

Lukwata, J. M. *Integrated African Liturgy*. Eldoret: AMECEA Gaba Publications, 2003.

Lumbala, Francois Kabasele. *Celebrating Jesus in Africa: Liturgy and Inculturation*. Maryknoll, NY: Orbis, 1998.

Luykx, Boniface. "The Impact of the Liturgical Documents". *African Ecclesiastical Review* (*AFER*) 13, no. 2 (April 1971): 97–107.

Magesa, L. *Anatomy of Inculturation: Transforming the Church in Africa*. Maryknoll, NY: Orbis, 2004.

———. "Theological Dialogue between the Christian Faith and African Culture". Unpublished paper presented to the Council of Anglican Provinces in Africa (CAPA) Theological Consultation on Wednesday, September 3, 2014.

Marshall, I. Howard. *Last Supper and Lord's Supper.* Carlisle: Paternoster, 1980.

Mbonigaba, G. Elisha. "The Indigenization of Liturgy". In *Anglican Liturgical Inculturation in Africa: The Kanamai Statement "African Culture and Anglican Liturgy"*. Edited by David Gitari, 20–32. Bramcote, Nottingham: Grove, 1994. An earlier version of this article can be found in *A Kingdom of Priests: Liturgical Formation of the People of God,* ed. Thomas J. Talley, 39–47. Bramcote, Nottingham: Grove, 1988.

McGrath, Alister. *Historical Theology.* Oxford: Blackwell, 1998.

Mulambuzi, X. F. "Beliefs in Ancestral Spirits: Interpreting Contemporary Attitudes of the Baganda to the Ancestors". Unpublished Master of Arts dissertation, Department of Religious Studies, University of Natal, 1997.

Ndung'u, Nahashon W. "Cultural Challenges and the Church in Africa". *African Ecclesiastical Review* (*AFER*) 50, no. 1–2 (March–June 2008): 71–94.

Nida, Eugene A. *Customs and Cultures: Anthropology for Christian Missions.* New York: Harper & Brothers, 1954.

Niebuhr, Richard H. *Christ and Culture.* London: Faber & Faber, 1952.

Nwagwu, Gerard. "A Canonical Perspective of Liturgical Inculturation in Africa". *African Ecclesiastical Review* (*AFER*) 43, no. 1–2 (February – April 2001): 56–65.

Oduro, Thomas. *Christ Holy Church International: The Story of an African Independent Church.* Lagos: Greater Heights Publishers, 2009.

Okonkwo, Izunna. "Eucharist and the African Communalism". *African Ecclesiastical Review* (*AFER*) 52, no. 2–3 (2010): 105–118.

———. "The Sacrament of the Eucharist (as Koinonia) and African Sense of Communalism: Towards a Synthesis". *Journal of Theology for Southern Africa* 137 (July 2010): 88–103.

Okoye, Chukwuma James. "Eucharist in African Perspective". *Mission Studies* 19, no. 1–2 (2002): 159–173.

———. "A Relevant African Eucharistic Celebration". *African Ecclesiastical Review (AFER)* 42, no. 5–6 (Oct–Dec 2000): 228–242.

———. "The Eucharist and African Culture". *African Ecclesiastical Review* (*AFER*) 34, no. 5 (October 1992): 272–292.

Olarewaju, Samuel. "The Efficacy of Prayer in the Blood of Christ in Contemporary African Christianity". *Africa Journal of Evangelical Theology* 22, no. 1 (2003): 31–49.

Power, N. David. *The Sacrifice We Offer: The Tridentine Dogma and Its Reinterpretations.* Edinburgh: T & T Clark, 1987.

Powers, M. Joseph. *Eucharistic Theology.* New York: Herder & Herder, 1967.

Priests of the Eastern Deanery of the Archdiocese of Nairobi. "Eucharistic Famine: A Pastoral Appeal to the 'Africa Synod'". *African Ecclesiastical Review (AFER)* 33, no. 4 (Aug 1991): 178–183.

Schineller, Peter. *A Handbook on Inculturation.* New York: Paulist, 1990.

Schweizer, E. *The Lord's Supper According to the New Testament.* Translation by James M. Davis. Philadelphia: Fortress, 1967.

———. "*Sarx*". In *Theological Dictionary of the New Testament*, vol. 7, edited by Gerhard Kittel and Gerhard Friedrich, 119–151. Grand Rapids, MI: Eerdmans, 1971.

Seasoltz, K. R. "Human Victimization and Christ as Victim in the Eucharist". *Worship* 76, no. 2 (March 2002): 98–124.

Shorter, A. "Three More African Eucharistic Prayers". *African Ecclesiastical Review (AFER)* 15 (1973): 152–160.

———. *Toward a Theology of Inculturation.* London: Geoffrey Chapman, 1988.

———. "Eucharistic Famine in Africa". *African Ecclesiastical Review* (*AFER*) 27, no. 3 (June 1985): 131–137.

———. "Liturgical Creativity in Africa". *African Ecclesiastical Review (AFER)* 5 (1977): 266.

Tovey, P. *Inculturation of Christian Worship: Exploring the Eucharist.* Aldershot, UK: Ashgate, 2004.

———. "The Symbol of the Eucharist in the African Context". Unpublished MPhil thesis, University of Nottingham, 1988.

Ukpong, Justin. "Inculturation and Evangelization: Biblical Foundations for Inculturation". In *Inculturation and Mission of the Church in Nigeria*, edited by Joseph Brookman-Amissah et al., 9–19. Port Harcourt: CIWA Press, 1992.

———. "Inculturation: A Major Challenge to the Church in Africa Today". *African Ecclesiastical Review* (*AFER*) 38, no. 5 (October 1996): 258–267.

———. "Christology and Inculturation: A New Testament Perspective". In *Paths of African Theology*, ed. Rosino Gibellini, 40–61. Maryknoll, NY: Orbis, 1994.

Uzukwu, Eugene. "Food and Drink in Africa, and the Christian Eucharist". *African Ecclesiastical Review* (*AFER*) 72 (1980): 370–385.

———. "Blessing and Thanksgiving among the Igbo (Nigeria): Towards an African Eucharistic Prayer". *African Ecclesiastical Review* (*AFER*) 72 (1980): 19.

———. *Liturgy: Truly Christian, Truly African.* Eldoret, Kenya: Gaba Publications, 1982.

———. "African Symbols and Christian Liturgical Celebration". *Worship* 65, no. 2 (1991): 98–112.

———. "Inculturation and the Liturgy (Eucharist)". In *Paths of African Theology*, ed. Rosino Gibellini, 95–114. Maryknoll, NY: Orbis 1994.

———. "Liturgy and Inculturation: A Century of Catholic Worship in Onitisha". *African Ecclesiastical Review* (*AFER*) 29, no. 1 (February 1987): 19–30.

Waliggo John Mary, Arij Roest Crollius, T. Nkeramihigo, and J. Mutiso-Mbinda. *Inculturation: Its Meaning and Urgency.* Nairobi: St. Paul Publications, 1986.

Wright, N. T. *Jesus and the Victory of God.* Minneapolis: Fortress, 1996.

Published Church Documents

A Modern Service of Holy Communion. Nairobi: Uzima Press, 1989.

Ekitabo Ky'omukristu. Kisubi: Marianum Press Kisubi, 1975.

Enneegayirira ezimu Ez'abakristu. 9th edition. Kisubi: Marianum Press Kisubi, 1990.

Luganda Prayer and Hymn Book. Kampala: Uganda Bookshop, 1977.

Provincial Canons of the Church of the Province of Uganda: Kampala: Centenary Publishing, 1997.

The Catechism of the Catholic Church. Nairobi: Pauline Publications – Africa, 1994.

The Practice and Procedure Manual of the Presbyterian Church of East Africa. 2nd edition. Nairobi: Publishing Solutions, 1998.

The Roman Catholic Code of Canon Law. New revised English translation. Bangalore: Theological Publications in India, 2004.

Unpublished Church Documents

Lambeth Conference 1908 Minutes V 3–5 August – 13th Day. Proceedings of the Fifth Lambeth Conference Monday 3rd August 1908 – Lambeth Library Archives document LC 70:19–39.

www.ingramcontent.com/pod-product-compliance
Ingram Content Group UK Ltd.
Pitfield, Milton Keynes, MK11 3LW, UK
UKHW020140250726
13967UKWH00002B/778

9 781783 684090